Also by Patrick Lencioni

The Ideal Team Player

HOW TO RECOGNIZE AND CULTIVATE THE THREE ESSENTIAL VIRTUES

A LEADERSHIP FABLE

Patrick Lencioni

A Wiley Brand

For general information about our other products and services, please contact our Customer Care Department within the United States at (800) 762-2974, outside the United States at (317) 572-3993 or fax (317) 572-4002.

Wiley publishes in a variety of print and electronic formats and by print-on-demand. Some material included with standard print versions of this book may not be included in e-books or in print-on-demand. If this book refers to media such as a CD or DVD that is not included in the version you purchased, you may download this material at http://booksupport.wiley.com. For more information about Wiley products, visit www.wiley.com.

ISBN 9781119209591 (cloth); ISBN 9781119209607 (ebk);
ISBN 9781119209614 (ebk)

Printed in the United States of America

SKY004003_083122

This is dedicated to Tracy Noble, who guided me through the process of writing this book, and who lives humble, hungry, and smart every day.

CONTENTS

INTRODUCTION

If someone were to ask me to make a list of the most valuable qualities a person should develop in order to thrive in the world of work—and for that matter, life—I would put being a team player at the top. The ability to work effectively with others, to add value within the dynamics of a group endeavor, is more critical in today's fluid world than it has ever been. Few people succeed at work, in the family, or in any social context without it.

I'm sure that most people would agree with this, which is why it's a little surprising that great team players are somewhat rare. I think the problem is that we've failed to define what being a team player requires, which leaves the concept somewhat vague, even soft.

It's not unlike teamwork itself, which still gets more lip service than practical attention. In my book, *The Five Dysfunctions of a Team*, I explained that real teamwork requires tangible, specific behaviors: vulnerability-based trust, healthy conflict, active commitment, peer-to-peer accountability, and a focus on results. Thankfully, with enough coaching, patience, and time, most people can learn to embrace those concepts.

However, I must admit that some people are better at being team players, at embracing those five behaviors, than others. They're not born that way, but either through life experiences, work history, or a real commitment to personal development, they come to possess the three underlying virtues that enable them to be ideal team players: they are humble, hungry, and smart. As simple as those words may appear, none of them is exactly what they seem. Understanding the nuances of these virtues is critical for applying them effectively.

During the past twenty years of working with leaders and their teams, I've seen time and again that when a team member lacks one or more of these three virtues, the process of building a cohesive team is much more difficult than it should be, and in some cases, impossible. We've been using this approach for hiring and management at The Table Group since our founding in 1997, and it has proven to be a remarkable predictor of success, as well as a reliable explanation of failure. As a result, we've come to the conclusion that these three seemingly obvious qualities are to teamwork what speed, strength, and coordination are to athletics—they make everything else easier.

The ramifications of all this are undeniable. Leaders who can identify, hire, and cultivate employees who are humble, hungry, and smart will have a serious advantage over those who cannot. They'll be able to build stronger teams much more quickly and with much less difficulty, and they'll significantly reduce the painful and tangible costs associated with politics, turnover, and morale problems. And employees who can embody these virtues will make themselves more valuable and marketable to any organization that values teamwork.

The purpose of this little book is to help you understand how the elusive combination of these three simple attributes can accelerate the process of making teamwork a reality in your organization or in your life so you can more effectively achieve the extraordinary benefits that it brings.

I hope it serves you well.

The Fable

PART ONE

The Situation

ENOUGH

After twenty years, Jeff Shanley had experienced more than his fair share of the Silicon Valley. The hours. The traffic. The pretentiousness. It was time to make a change.

To be fair, it wasn't really the work that Jeff had grown tired of. In fact, he had enjoyed an interesting and successful career. After a few jobs in high-tech marketing, at age thirty-five he cofounded a technology start-up. Two years later, he was fortunate enough to get demoted when the board of directors hired what they called a grown-up CEO. During the next four years, that CEO, Kathryn Petersen, taught Jeff more about leadership, teamwork, and business than he could have learned in a decade of business school.

When Kathryn retired, Jeff left the company and spent the next few years working at a small consulting firm in Half Moon Bay, over the hills from the Silicon Valley. Jeff thrived there, and was on the verge of becoming a partner. But during that time, he and his wife began to grow tired of trying to keep up with the Joneses, which happened to be the name of the family that lived in the over-priced bungalow next door.

Jeff was definitely ready for a change. Where he would go and what he would do next was a mystery to him. He certainly didn't expect the answer to come via a phone call from his uncle Bob.

BOB

Robert Shanley had been the most prominent and diversified building contractor in the Napa Valley for three decades. Whether it was a winery, a school, or a shopping center, if it was being built in Napa, there was a decent chance that Valley Builders was involved in some significant way.

Unfortunately for Bob, none of his kids was interested in taking over the family business, instead choosing to be restauranteurs, stockbrokers, and high school teachers. And that's why Bob called his nephew to see if he knew anyone who might be interested in running the company in a couple of years when Bob retired.

It wasn't the first time that Bob had turned to his nephew for advice. Jeff had helped him on a few occasions in the past, and actually consulted to the executive team a year earlier on a substantial project around teamwork, which was one of the firm's values. Jeff had focused his efforts on building more effective teams at the highest levels of the company.

Bob loved the work Jeff did, and often bragged about his nephew during family reunions, usually saying something to the effect of "this boy is my best advisor." His cousins teased Jeff, pretending to resent their father's favoritism.

Bob thought so much of Jeff that he had absolutely no expectation that his ambitious nephew in the exciting world of high tech would ever be interested in working in construction. Which is why he was so stunned when Jeff asked, "Would you consider hiring someone without industry experience? Someone like me?"

TRANSITION

Within the month, Jeff and Maurine Shanley had sold their tiny home in San Mateo and moved their two children and one dog to the northern end of Napa—the town, not the valley. Jeff's commute to the Valley Builders office was about four miles, and even if he drove the speed limit, it took just seven minutes.

It was during those minutes that Jeff experienced an initial wave of remorse. Though everything on the domestic side of his decision had been going well, learning the nuances of the construction industry proved to be more of a challenge than he expected. Or, more precisely, it was the lack of nuance that was the problem.

Everything in construction seemed to come down to physical, material issues. Gone were the days of theoretical debates and pie-in-the-sky planning. Jeff now found himself learning about concrete matters having to do with everything from air conditioning to lumber to, well, concrete.

But soon enough, Jeff not only got used to this new way of working, he actually came to prefer it. Straightforward conversations about tangible things may have been less sophisticated than high tech, but they were also more gratifying.

And he was learning more than he could have imagined from his uncle, who never finished college but seemed to have a better understanding of business than many of the CEOs Jeff had worked with in technology.

After eight weeks of observation and learning, Jeff came to the conclusion that the move to Napa was the right one and that the stress of his previous life in the Silicon Valley was over.

He was wrong.

PART TWO

Diagnosis

THE ROPES

ob Shanley had never been a cautious man, which was one of the reasons his firm had done so well. He had been decisive and bold in growing the company when others were hedging their bets. Aside from the occasional and inevitable economic downturns, most of Bob's decisions had yielded significant long-term benefits.

The firm had more than two hundred people on staff, making it one of the larger employers in the area. Those employees, ranging from entry-level construction workers to architectural engineers, were generally well compensated and, more important to Bob, had generous benefits plans. Though bonuses varied from year to year depending on the region's economy and the success of Bob's business development, no one who worked at Valley Builders felt underpaid.

Employees weren't the only people who depended on VB's financial success. A small group of family members, whom Bob called "private shareholders," had a financial stake in the company. These were Bob's wife and kids, as well as a few of his siblings who helped him launch the company more than three decades earlier. One of those siblings was

Jeff's dad, who had relied on the financial windfall to help fund his retirement.

During those first months on the job, Jeff had focused almost exclusively on learning the operations of construction. This consisted primarily of studying the day-to-day tactical and financial nature of the business, everything from materials acquisition and scheduling to permitting and labor costs. Bob decided to wait a few months to teach Jeff about the longer-term strategic issues related to the company's overall financial health and new business development. Though Jeff certainly asked a few questions about those issues, Bob assured him that he would sit down with Jeff to review that part of the business as soon as his nephew felt comfortable in the blocking and tackling of the construction industry.

Jeff had no idea how soon that day would come and what a shock that conversation would be. For that matter, neither did Bob.

DISCLOSURE

itting down for lunch at an upscale BBQ restaurant near the Napa River, Bob got right to the point.

"Here's the deal. I am ridiculously happy that I hired you. You've already been a blessing to me and the company."

Jeff felt as gratified by this feedback as any he had heard in his career, probably because it came from a family member. But he could tell his uncle had more to say.

"In fact, I'm not going to wait a year to put you in charge. We're going to do it right away."

Caught completely off guard by the announcement, Jeff pushed back. "Whoa. I don't think we should get ahead of—"

Smiling, Bob waved his hand and interrupted. "Don't start telling me you're not ready, because I already know that."

Jeff was confused.

"I don't want you to be ready, Jeff. I want you to be excited. And a little nervous. That's good for you."

Something about his uncle seemed off to Jeff. "Well, I think I'll be plenty excited and nervous in six months. Why don't we just—"

"Because we can't," Bob interrupted again, this time in a much more serious tone. He paused and struggled to get out the next sentence. "Jeff, my doctor says I have a serious heart condition. The kind you don't recover from. I don't understand half the words the doctor uses. Something about ischemia and angina. All I know is that he says I need surgery and that my life needs to change. Immediately."

Just then the waitress shattered the moment when she came over to take their orders. Recovering himself immediately, Bob promptly ordered a salad with no dressing and a glass of water. Then he teased Jeff.

"But if you don't get the ribs, I'm going to kick your ass right here."

Jeff laughed, and ordered the ribs. As the waitress walked away, he asked Bob the big question: "Are you going to be okay?"

"If surgery goes well and I do what the doctor tells me, I should be fine. But it's going to be hard for me. Which is why I have to step away from the business." Bob paused. "I can't believe I just said that. I think I'm still in shock that I won't be there next week. But I have to leave, because I'm not good at doing things halfway."

"When is your surgery?"

"A week from tomorrow, unless something changes and they can get me in sooner."

Jeff was stunned.

Though he was showing his trademark confidence and humor, Bob was clearly taking all of this very seriously.

"Honestly, Jeff, I don't know what we'd do if we hadn't hired you."

Jeff nodded, glad for the confidence but not loving the context of it all. That context was about to get much worse.

WHEN IT RAINS

Jeff decided to dive into the details. "Well, I hate to do this, but I think it's time we talked about the balance sheet and the longer-term financials of the company."

Bob nodded a little sheepishly and reached for something in his computer bag. "I think I've brought most of what you need."

Knowing his uncle well, Jeff was starting to feel like something wasn't right. He probed. "Based on everything I've seen so far, I'm guessing the company's in pretty good shape." It was more of a question than a statement.

Bob smiled, the same way he used to smile when he assured the kids he wouldn't throw them in the deep end of the pool just before he did exactly that. "Absolutely." He didn't sound confident. "But I need to talk to you about some new challenges and opportunities."

As concerned as he was, Jeff laughed out loud. "I don't think I like the sound of this."

"Oh, you'll be fine. This is just how the industry works."

The waitress brought Jeff's beer and Bob's water.

"So what kind of challenges and opportunities are we talking about?" Jeff asked.

Bob stopped rifling through his bag and looked Jeff in the eye with a bizarre mix of excitement and worry.

"Jeff, we just landed two great projects."

He paused to let his nephew take in the information, and then continued.

"It's very exciting. The Queen of the Valley Hospital project, which I mentioned to you a few weeks ago, came through on Monday. And I signed the papers yesterday morning for the new hotel project in St. Helena." He paused and seemed to force a big smile. "We're going to build both of them."

Jeff was confused. "That's good news, right?"

"It's fantastic news," Bob answered, in a tone that was something less than fantastic.

"When was the last time we had two projects like that on the books at the same time?" Jeff was more than a little curious to know.

Bob hesitated, looking down at his glass of water for a moment and back up at Jeff. "That's the thing. We've never had two major projects like this at the same time." He paused. "In fact, both of these are as big as anything we've ever done."

Any semblance of a smile that had remained on Jeff's face disappeared. As overwhelmed as he was, he had yet to receive the worst news of all.

COMMITTED

Jeff took a deep breath. "Okay. I know this is hard to hear, and the last thing I want to do is stress you out, Bob. But maybe we need to focus on one of the projects and let the other one go. I mean, it sounds like this would be a challenge if you were running the show, but with a new and inexperienced CEO like me, this could be a recipe for disaster."

Bob nodded and took a drink of his water. "I understand."

Jeff wanted to be relieved, but he sensed that a qualifier was coming. He was right.

His uncle's smile slid into a wince. "It's just that the legal nature of the hospital deal is that if we back out, we lose a huge chunk of capital. And they've already advanced us a first payment on the hotel, part of which we're using to finish the Oak Ridge shopping center."

Jeff was now starting to feel very warm, and not in a good way. He took a long drink from the beer bottle in front of him. "So we're talking about cash flow issues? And this is too much to walk away from?"

Bob nodded. "Oh yeah. It would be a deal breaker for the firm." Then his smile returned. "But as soon as we get these projects going, we'll be fine from a cash standpoint."

Suddenly, Jeff was not appreciating his uncle so much.

Bob tried to cheer him up. "You can do this, Jeff. You're smarter than I am. You're younger than I am. And you'll have plenty of help."

Jeff's tone changed. "How long ago did this all happen?" He was beginning to sound a little accusatory.

"Well, like I said, the hotel deal closed yesterday, and the hospital came through—"

"No, I mean with the doctor?" Jeff interrupted.

Bob was puzzled. "Well, that was just yesterday afternoon. It was supposed to be just a precautionary test because I had a little pain recently." His eyes opened widely as he suddenly realized what Jeff was getting at. "You don't think that I knew all this and set you up, do you? I wouldn't do that to you, Jeff."

Bob started to sound a little choked up. "If I had any idea that I'd be leaving the business, I would never have agreed to these projects and put you in this dilemma."

Jeff felt terrible for his uncle and for having seemed to distrust him. But he couldn't help but ask the next question: "So then you *don't* think I can do it?"

"No, that's not what I meant. I just meant that putting you in a situation like this is not something I would have done on purpose. But that doesn't mean you can't manage it. You'll hire a few more people. It's just a matter of scale. It will be fine."

Jeff hoped Bob really meant it. He wasn't convinced.

THE PLUNGE

Jeff decided not to finish the rest of his beer. He figured he'd need to get back to work and be focused for the rest of the day, and probably into the evening.

Bob told his nephew that he had already informed his two most senior people of the impending change, and he advised Jeff to go see them right after lunch. Jeff agreed, and then asked whether he would have complete freedom in running the company.

Bob assured him. "No limits or restrictions. Starting immediately."

Glad to have that assurance, Jeff spent the rest of lunch talking with his uncle about his health and his family. No business at all. At the end of the conversation, as he stood to leave, he apologized for questioning Bob's intent.

"I don't blame you," Bob assured him. "I'd have wondered the same thing."

Suddenly, Bob smiled and looked at Jeff intently. "You know something? One of the worst things about all this is that I'm not going to get to work with you." He paused to avoid getting emotional. "You might not know this, but I've been more excited these past couple months than I have been in years."

Jeff gave his dad's brother the kind of hug that had nothing to do with business and left the restaurant with a heavy heart.

On his way back to the VB offices, he called the two executives he would be relying on to keep the company alive, and scheduled a meeting that afternoon. One of the reasons he hadn't lost all hope in his future at the firm was his confidence in two long-time employees, Clare Massick and Bobby Brady.

Clare was a tallish blonde woman a few years younger than Jeff who ran all of the firm's administration, which included finance, legal, and HR. She had been the only human resources leader in the company's history, hired begrudgingly seven years earlier after Bob's personal attorney convinced him that not having an HR function was exposing the company from a legal standpoint. Bob insisted on finding someone who would be supportive of the company and interested in construction. As he explained it to the candidates he interviewed, "I don't want some tree-hugging activist who hates business coming in here and screwing up the culture."

Many of those candidates opted out of the process, but when Clare heard those words, she knew she belonged. The daughter of a military dad and a dance teacher mom, she had struggled to find her calling after college. Fascinated by psychology and business, but not enough to pursue a career in either field on its own, she decided that human resources might provide her with the right combination.

Her first several years in HR prior to joining VB were horrendous—a mix of bureaucratic protocol and touchy-feely workshops. Clare was all but ready to bail from the field when she heard about the job opening at Valley Builders. After 20 minutes with Bob Shanley, Clare had a change of heart.

Jeff had come to know Clare over the past few years, especially through his teamwork consulting engagement with VB. During the executive team sessions, he had quickly learned why Bob liked her and why he had put so much responsibility in her hands. Thankfully, she seemed glad when Jeff joined the company, so he figured they would work well together.

Bobby Brady, a smiling, barrel-chested, fifty-two-year-old with graying hair, was the head of all field operations at VB. He had first proved his good nature eleven years earlier when he arrived at the firm and his peers decided that it would be too confusing to have two Bobs on the leadership team. So, in a moment of playful cruelty, they referred to him as Bobby, knowing full well that this was the name of the youngest boy character on *The Brady Bunch*, one of America's most iconic sitcoms.

Bob, or Bobby, didn't blink, embracing the moniker with self-deprecating humor and unexpected grace, deciding that he would be able to discard the name before long. Much to his surprise, he quickly grew accustomed to his new identity at work, and found that it helped him build relationships with contractors and vendors who liked to tease him.

It certainly helped that Bobby knew the construction business cold. He had built a solid reputation in his career for being honest, diligent, and timely in his projects—something that set him apart from many of his peers in the industry.

When Jeff called Clare and Bobby on the way back to the office to ask them to meet with him in Bob's office, he learned that Bob had broken the big news to them just a few hours earlier over breakfast. Jeff was more than a little curious to find out what Clare and Bobby thought of the new arrangement after only a few hours to digest it. Their reactions would not be what he expected.

DRAMA

hen Jeff arrived, Clare and Bobby were already in his uncle's office, an unspectacular room that Bob refused to modernize or decorate since the company was founded. His wife referred to its style as "1970s Construction," which suited her husband just fine.

Bobby was sitting behind the big wooden desk, and he didn't look happy.

"Sit down, Jeff." It felt like an order.

Clare went first. "Jeff, I think you know that we're not the kind of people who smile at someone in person and then talk about them behind their backs. We're going to be up front with you, whether you like it or not."

Before Jeff could say *sure*, Bobby took over.

"The thing is, we're not too thrilled about you being our new boss."

Jeff froze. He would tell his wife later that night that he felt like he was in a scene from a bad movie.

Bobby paused to let the words hang there before continuing. "I've worked my ass off for more than a decade for your blowhard uncle, and how does he reward me? By giving the top job to his nephew?"

25

Jeff was stunned, and looked at Clare to see if she shared any of his shock at the harsh words coming out of Bobby's mouth. Apparently she didn't, because she just stared at Jeff, who tried to defend himself.

"Listen, I didn't expect—"

Bobby interrupted him. "I don't want to hear it. You knew when you came here that you had the inside track. Bob must have known when he hired you that he'd be leaving."

"No, he said that he just met with the doctor yesterday, and that he—"

Now Clare interrupted. "Come on, Jeff. Do you think we were born yesterday?"

It seemed like Clare had more to say, but she suddenly stopped, stood up, and turned away from Jeff toward the windows.

Bobby looked at her with a mix of concern and disappointment on his face. With greater intensity than before, he continued the tirade directed at Jeff. "So here's the deal. If you're going to be the boss, we're out of here."

Jeff was spinning. Speechless.

As angry as he should have been, Bobby seemed distracted by Clare, glancing over at her.

Jeff turned to see why and noticed that Clare was visibly shaking.

Is she crying? He wondered.

"Good luck making this place work on your own, buddy!" Bobby stood and moved toward the door. "Let's go, Clare."

And that's when Clare seemed to break. Bending over to put her face in her hands, she started shaking even more.

Jeff was as confused as ever.

And that's when he heard the sound of Clare choking back laughter.

"Shit, Clare!" Bobby shouted at his colleague.

She turned toward Bobby and broke down laughing. "I'm sorry, I just couldn't."

"You blew it! We had him going!" Bobby was shaking his head at Clare.

Finally, Jeff came to terms with the prank that had just been pulled on him.

"You guys are bastards!" Jeff's indignation was more than tempered by his relief. Smiling, he picked up a bottle of water from the table in front of him and threw it at Bobby, who caught it.

"Admit it. We got you," Bobby teased.

"I'm so sorry, Jeff," Clare pleaded with her new boss. "He made me do it."

Jeff teased her. "So, I guess you'll be handling your own termination?"

She winced. "Bob is going to be so pissed at us when he hears about this."

"No he's not," Bobby countered. "He'll think it's hilarious."

Jeff agreed with him. "Yeah, he will. The blowhard."

GALLOWS HUMOR

Clare then tried to sober the room. "Why are we laughing? We're all screwed."

This only made them laugh harder for a moment, until reality began to take hold.

Jeff felt like the situation was a little morose, given his uncle's medical condition. "Do you guys think he's going to be okay?"

Suddenly Clare felt bad for her new boss. "Oh yeah, I do. Tell him what you said earlier, Bobby."

"My brother had the same diagnosis a few years ago, and the same surgery. It's not all that risky, as long as his diet and lifestyle change." Bobby paused to let Jeff digest it all. "He should be fine."

Glad for their reassurance about his uncle, Jeff needed a little for himself, too.

"So, is there any truth, even a little, to what you guys were saying?" Before they could answer, he explained. "I mean, do you guys feel like one of you should have gotten this job?"

Jeff was glad that Bobby went first. "Are you kidding? If Bob had made me CEO I'd have quit. I know what I'm good at, and it's not this," he said, looking around the office. "I'm a field ops guy."

Clare jumped in. "And as much as I've loved advising Bob, I wouldn't be right in that chair. That's not for me."

"Okay, but how do you feel about me sitting in it?"

"Well, we'd be lying if we didn't admit that we had concerns," Clare said, with a perfect combination of bluntness and compassion.

Bobby continued, "Oh yeah. We're as worried as you are, my friend. But it's not like we had someone else in mind who we think would be better. Given the craziness of the situation right now, you're probably our best option."

"Why do you say that?"

Clare answered, "Because we need someone we know and trust. There's no hero out there who could come in from the outside and make this work. And you're invested. You're family."

"And you're not a jackass," Bobby announced, without a hint of humor. "You're a good kid, and you listen. We know you get us."

Jeff could never have imagined that the words "you're not a jackass" could be so comforting. Or that he'd be considered a kid in his forties. Still, he had to push a little harder.

"Okay, I appreciate that. But I have to ask the big question." He paused for effect. "Are you ready to let me be the leader of the company? And of you guys?"

Clare and Bobby looked at each other, and then turned to Jeff.

"Absolutely," Bobby declared.

Clare agreed. "Same here."

Jeff was relieved. "Okay. You up for dinner tonight?"

FIRST MEETING

Sitting down at a big table in the back of Maria's Mexican Restaurant a few blocks from the office, Jeff and his new direct reports moved aside their plates and silverware to make room for paperwork. Given that it was a weeknight and that the food at Maria's wasn't particularly good, they had much of the establishment to themselves.

"Okay, let's try to avoid getting into too many details right now," Jeff explained. "Let's just identify the biggest levers that we're going to need to pull to make this work."

Bobby and Clare didn't respond right away, so he clarified.

"I'm talking about big categories. Like financing. Labor. Materials."

Now their heads were nodding, and almost in unison they said "labor."

His mouth full, Jeff motioned for them to explain, and Bobby went first.

"We need to add at least," he paused to do some quick math in his head, "sixty people in the next two months." He looked at Clare for confirmation.

She sighed, agreeing.

"What kind of people are we talking about?" Jeff wanted to know. "Nail pounders? Project managers? Foremen?"

"Yes," Bobby responded with no sense of humor. "Everything."

Clare added, "But there are four critical hires we have to make first. A project manager for the hospital, two foremen, and a senior engineer."

"Three foremen," Bobby corrected her.

"Okay, maybe three foremen. And then we're going to need a half dozen supervisors and about fifty contractors, of all kinds." She shook her head as if she hadn't quite realized the gravity of the situation until going over the list. "This is crazy."

Jeff wrote the numbers in a notepad.

They spent the next thirty minutes talking about the specific jobs they'd need to fill and how they would deploy them.

Jeff decided it was time to move on. "Okay, what else, besides hiring?"

For almost two hours, the three executives went through the details of the two big projects, everything from permits and schedules to design and materials.

Jeff thought he had learned a lot in his first sixty days on the job, but he would later admit that he absorbed more during those three hours at Maria's than in the previous two months. It was like a crash course in construction management, inspired by the new sense of urgency. And fear.

At nine o'clock, he decided to call it a night. "Let's not burn ourselves out on the first leg of this race."

They agreed to meet the next afternoon after Bobby came back from the Oak Ridge building site, a problematic shopping center project that VB was trying to finish.

REGROUPING

On the way home, Jeff called Uncle Bob's youngest son, Ben. He had always been Jeff's favorite cousin for the same reason that Bob was his favorite uncle. Ben shared his dad's big personality, though not his girth.

Ben was a history teacher and basketball coach at a high school up in the valley in St. Helena. Though he was barely forty, he had become something of a legend as a coach, whose teams always seemed to win more than their talent warranted.

Jeff decided he wouldn't even touch on business issues, not wanting to be insensitive. "How are you feeling about your dad's situation?"

Ben didn't seem overly concerned. "I'm okay. I'm just glad he found out when he did. Based on what the doctor said, he should be okay, as long as he stops eating all that crap and stays out of the work stress. Frankly, I'm probably more worried about you."

"Me?" Jeff was genuinely surprised.

"Yeah, with Dad stepping away, I'm wondering how you're feeling. And what you think's going to happen at VB."

For a moment, Jeff wondered whether Ben was more concerned about his cousin or his own financial interests.

"Well, it's going to be hard, but after meeting with Clare and Bobby tonight, I think we'll figure it out." Jeff was acting more confident than he was feeling.

"I wish I could help." Ben seemed sincere.

"Well, I'll take all the help I can get. Do you have any opinions or ideas about the business?"

"I'm afraid I don't know much about the Xs and Os of what Dad does. I wish I did. But if you want to put together a company basketball team, I'm your man."

Jeff laughed. "All right. Hey, if there is anything I can ever do for your mom and dad, let me know."

"I will. Main thing is to keep them in your prayers."

"You know I will."

Ben smiled. "We all really appreciate what you're doing for Dad. The company means a lot to the family, and not just financially."

"Of course," Jeff replied, doing his best to mask the growing pressure he was feeling.

The cousins agreed to get together for coffee in a week, and the conversation ended just as Jeff pulled into his driveway.

He hadn't talked to his wife, Maurine, since all of this happened, wanting to break the news to her in person. She was a constant source of perspective and empathy, as well as optimism. Usually, Jeff appreciated that optimism. Tonight he was more than a little disappointed that she didn't seem even a little worried.

"As bad as I feel for Bob, I think the work part is actually a good thing for you," Maurine explained.

Jeff looked at her like she was insane.

She clarified. "Just listen. I love that it's calmer up here and that your commute is shorter and that we see you more. But you need a challenge. You've always needed challenges."

"I don't know." He took a deep breath. "This one might be a little too close to home."

She seemed a little surprised. "You mean the family thing?"

He nodded. "I never thought that my success at work could impact my relationship with my family. Heck, even my dad will know if I screw this up."

Maurine dismissed it all. "Don't be silly. They're all rooting for you. No one expects you to be Superman. Just take it one issue at a time."

Jeff wanted to argue, but knew that she was right. Thinking about the big picture too much would overwhelm him, but he could certainly manage one issue at a time.

Fortunately, the first and most important issue would be the subject of his meeting the next day.

GETTING MESSY

Jeff took a detour on his way to work in the morning, stopping by the Oak Ridge building site to check in with Bobby and his crew. When he pulled up to the trailer, he didn't see Bobby's car.

"He left five minutes ago," someone standing outside the VB trailer explained.

Jeff decided to spend some time walking the site, greeting as many workers as he could find, just to get a better sense of who they were. It certainly wasn't the first time since joining the company that he had been to a work site; he had made a habit of going into the field a few times every week. But he had never been to Oak Ridge, mostly because it was almost complete and provided few learning opportunities compared to the earlier-stage projects. But Jeff was learning new things now and viewing the site from a CEO's perspective, even if no one knew that he was their new boss.

When he arrived back at the office, Bobby and Clare were sitting at Uncle Bob's desk.

"Hey, I thought you were going to spend the morning at Oak Ridge," Jeff said to Bobby. "I guess I missed you by a few minutes."

Clare carried her open laptop over to Jeff and put it in front of him. "You need to read this. We're sending it out this morning," she explained, a little sadly.

Jeff was confused. "Okay." He sat down to read an e-mail that Bob had written to his employees. It was a touching explanation of his medical situation, his fondness for VB and the people who worked there, and his sadness about having to leave. Jeff had tears in his eyes within minutes. Bob also announced that he was extremely glad to name Jeff as the company's new leader. He even noted that Clare and Bobby had expressed to him their confidence in Jeff, both as a person and as an executive.

When Jeff finished, he looked up at Bobby and Clare, who seemed at once to be melancholy about Bob and concerned for the company.

"Bob wanted to send a video," Clare explained, "but he decided he wouldn't be able to get through it because he'd be too emotional."

"And just in case you're wondering, he was telling the truth about our confidence in you," Bobby added without much emotion.

Jeff was overwhelmed, mostly by gratitude, but by pressure, too. He would never forget that moment.

Thankfully, Clare broke the silence.

"Okay, boys. We need to get to work." She paused and took a deep breath. "So what's going on at Oak Ridge, Bobby?"

"Things looked okay today. Which is why I came here early. I figured we should get started as soon as possible."

Jeff moved to his desk and opened his notebook. "Alright then. Let's talk about staffing." He looked at his notes. "Basically, we have eight weeks to hire sixty people."

Bobby winced. "Ooh. Don't say eight weeks. Call it two months. That sounds longer." Then he corrected his boss. "And it's more like eighty people."

Jeff was confused, looking down at his notebook. "Wait. Last night you said sixty."

Clare explained. "We said we need sixty more people to staff the project. To do that we'll have to hire at least eighty."

"Why?"

"We'll lose at least twenty of them along the way."

Jeff was shocked. "That's thirty-three percent turnover."

"We can do math, too, smart guy," Bobby teased him.

Jeff looked at Clare. "Is that typical for every construction company? Why haven't I heard about this sooner?"

She explained, "Turnover in construction isn't uncommon. But we're higher than most."

"Why?"

"Because we're a little more demanding of our employees when it comes to behavior. Bob just doesn't tolerate people who don't fit the VB culture."

"You mean teamwork?" Jeff asked.

Clare and Bobby nodded.

Jeff decided to let the turnover issue go for the moment. "Okay," he sighed, "where do we find these people? Let's start with the guys pounding nails and pouring cement."

Clare waved off the question. "We've got that covered. We have sources, and if we have to, we can staff the lower-level jobs through subcontractors and temp services. It'll cost us more, but that's a high class problem at this point."

"And what about the foremen and the project manager?"

"Well, that's a little harder. And we just lost two foremen a few months ago, so we're already a little behind."

"Yeah, what happened with that?"

"Well, you know that Oak Ridge is almost a month late, which isn't as bad as it could have been, given the problems we had. Two of our best foremen quit because the conditions on site were toxic."

Jeff looked worried. "You don't mean literally toxic."

"No, I mean ugly. We had a difficult project manager handling one part of the job and a few pushy foremen who made things worse. Life was pretty miserable over there for a while."

"How so?"

Bobby jumped in. "Bullshit accusations from one group to another, mostly about who was slacking off and who was pulling their weight."

"What about the difficult project manager? What did he do?"

"She," Clare explained. "Nancy Morris. She tried to ignore it. Told everyone to just get along and get their work done. Things got worse."

"Who got fired?" Jeff wanted to know.

"Well," Bobby explained a little sheepishly, "no one. When the two foremen quit, we couldn't afford to lose anyone, even if we wanted to. It was a total mess."

Jeff tried not to sound judgmental. "So, are we planning to keep the crappy project manager and foremen?"

"Unfortunately, yes," Bobby answered. "We're going to need as many people as we can get."

Now Jeff couldn't hold back his frustration. "So, I guess the teamwork stuff we did last year wasn't real after all."

Clare was defensive now. "Wait. That's not fair. Bob was very serious about it, and so were we. He always says that he'd rather sell the company than have a bunch of political, self-centered people working here."

Bobby added, "And it wasn't just a bunch of bullshit posters and T-shirts, if that's what you mean. We did those sessions on trust and healthy conflict and accountability, the ones you helped us with. We just got busy and dropped the ball, and didn't push it down into the rest of the organization. That was probably my bad, because most of these people worked in my group."

"I should've seen it sooner, too," Clare admitted.

Jeff wasn't convinced, but tried to stay focused. "Where did the two foremen go? The ones who left."

"They're doing contract work on the other end of the valley," Bobby explained. "Residential stuff."

"Are they really good? And if so, can we get them back?"

Bobby shrugged. "I'm not sure."

Jeff frowned. "You mean you're not sure if they're good or not?"

Bobby shook his head. "No, I don't know if we can get them back. As far as whether they're good, I guess it depends on what you mean by good."

"Well, how about in terms of teamwork?" Jeff asked, looking at Clare.

She shrugged. "That probably depends on who you ask, too, but I thought they were solid."

Jeff was more than a little troubled by the lack of clarity from his colleagues, and decided he didn't have the luxury of holding back.

THE HAMMER

"Okay, I'm going to get pretty direct here, if that's alright." Jeff was trying hard to be polite.

Bobby and Clare looked at each other with a little concern on their faces, and then they nodded.

"You guys, and Bob, really dropped the ball on the teamwork project."

They didn't say anything, so Jeff continued, focusing on Bobby. "You said it wasn't just posters and T-shirts, but what else was it?" Before they could answer, he went on. "Because you don't seem to know what you mean when you talk about team players. And so you can't possibly know who needs to change, who should stay, and who should go."

"We didn't say—" Clare wanted to explain, but Jeff wouldn't let her.

"Oh wait. I forgot." Jeff was being sarcastic, but not rude. "You do have one clear definition. A person can't be a jackass."

They laughed, but in a guilty sort of way.

After a moment, Bobby said something surprising.

"Actually, that's probably about right. Call them jerks or SOBs. Whatever the case, that's how I think about it."

Jeff smiled. "Let's stick with jackasses for right now. So, how do you know if a person is a jackass? And how do you avoid hiring them?"

Clare answered first. "I guess you know one after you've worked with one for a while."

Jeff shook his head. "Yeah, but by then it's too late. And you know what happens when you keep a jackass longer than you should?"

They didn't respond, so he answered the question for them. "The non-jackasses start to leave."

He might as well have punched Bobby in the stomach, because the look on his face was a pained one.

Looking at Clare, Bobby declared, "That's what happened with Carl and Pedro."

Clare explained it to Jeff. "They're the two foremen we lost. I don't know about Carl, but Pedro definitely wasn't a jackass. Nancy and some of the others on her team, I'm not too sure about."

"You guys see the problem, right?"

They nodded, and Clare made a sarcastic suggestion. "Maybe our new slogan should be 'no jackasses allowed.' That would make a great poster."

Bobby picked up his pen and started to write. "I'll get right on that. Is jackass one word or two?"

Ignoring her colleague's humor, Clare seemed to have a revelation. "You know, we always just relied on Bob for knowing who fit and who didn't. He had a way with sizing people up. But even he couldn't get everyone right. And he couldn't interview and decide on every candidate at every level. I guess it just broke down."

Jeff seemed suddenly energized. "Well, I think it's time we figured this out. We have to stop hiring people who aren't team players. And we have to find out how many non–team players are still working here, and then get them to change or move them out."

He paused and looked at his notes. "Because if we can't do that, I don't see how we're going to build a hotel and new wing on a hospital in the next eighteen months." He paused, and took a breath. "And as much as I hate to say it, if we can't do that, then I really don't know how we're going to keep VB in business."

RESEARCH

Jeff decided to go back to the Oak Ridge site during lunch, "to take another look with a different set of eyes," as he explained it to Clare and Bobby.

On the way, he called his cousin, Ben.

"Hey, remember when I said we should have coffee next week?" He didn't wait for an answer. "How about this afternoon instead?"

Ben teased him. "You really miss me, don't you?"

"You know I do. And maybe I can ask you some questions."

"About the company?"

"Kind of. But not really. I'll explain it when I see you. Does three thirty work for you?"

"How about four? I've got office hours until three forty-five."

"See you at Starbucks. The one by the A&W restaurant off the highway."

By the time he hung up, he was pulling up to the new Oak Ridge shopping center. *I love how close everything is up here*, he thought.

Because construction crews start working earlier than most people, they eat lunch earlier, too. Though it was just past noon, everyone was back on the job, so Jeff went to the trailer to see who was there. Nancy Morris was sitting at the makeshift desk in the corner of the sparse trailer, rifling through papers.

"Excuse me," Jeff interrupted her.

Nancy looked up, but didn't say anything.

"Hi, I'm Jeff."

She responded as though he were a cement vendor. "Yeah, I know. We met once at the office. Come on in." She motioned to a folding chair on the other side of her desk, but couldn't seem to break a smile. "I guess I should congratulate you on your promotion."

"Well, I wish it would have been under different circumstances, but thank you."

"How can I help you?" Nancy asked without emotion.

"Well, I was just wondering if you're a jackass."

Jeff didn't actually say that, but that's what he was thinking. Instead, he decided to take a more subtle approach. "How are things going around here?"

Nancy continued looking through her papers while she answered. "Well, it depends on what you mean."

Jeff was a little surprised by her abruptness and a little intimidated in a way he hadn't experienced in high tech.

Nancy was attractive, about Jeff's age, and almost a foot shorter than him. Still, Jeff decided she could probably take him in a wrestling match. It wasn't her size or apparent strength, but rather her demeanor—a mix of toughness and self-confidence.

Jeff knew this was no time to be weak. "Well, for starters, how confident are you that we're going to make the new deadline?"

"My part of it looks good, but you'll have to ask Craig. He's the other project manager doing the hardscaping and civic stuff."

"So you don't know how he's doing?"

She shook her head. "Not really. Haven't seen him much lately."

Jeff didn't want to have this conversation, but couldn't let it go. "Nancy, it seems to me that you ought to know about the entire project. If we miss another deadline, it's not going to matter which part is late."

Nancy looked up and took a breath. "Listen, Craig doesn't even invite me to his meetings anymore. So I just keep my head down, work my tail off, and leave it at that. I really do want to get this project done on time, but it's been pretty awful, and I'll be glad when it's over. I'm sorry if that sounds bad, but it's my reality right now."

Part of Jeff appreciated her honesty, but a bigger part thought she was just abrasive.

"Do you know where I can find Craig?"

She shook her head. "No. But if I had to guess, I'd say he's over by the main entrance to the parking lot. I saw him there about an hour ago."

Jeff left, knowing he'd have to address Nancy's issues at some point. He wasn't looking forward to that day.

TWO SIDES

Jeff happened to know what Craig looked like because their kids went to the same school and they had a couple beers together at the annual St. Mary's Parish International Night a few weeks earlier.

Craig noticed Jeff walking toward him and broke away from the workers he was standing with near the entrance.

"Well, two visits in one day," he said, smiling. "Everything okay?"

Jeff was glad that Craig seemed happy to see him. "Yeah, everything's fine. I just wanted to know how things are going." Suddenly, deciding that he should be more direct, Jeff corrected himself. "Actually, maybe things aren't fine. I don't know."

Craig looked concerned. "How can I help?"

"Well, I was just talking to Nancy, and it seems like you guys have had some issues." Before Craig could jump in, Jeff continued. "Now, I know about the foremen who quit a few months ago, and all that. Bobby gave me the basic story there. I'm just wondering what your take is, and why you and Nancy aren't working better together."

Craig frowned. "How frank do you want me to be?"

"Does anyone ever say not to be frank?"

"I guess not." Craig smiled. "But I could give you the politically correct answer, or I could cut to the chase."

"The chase."

"Okay, that woman," he said, pointing to the trailer across the parking lot, "has some serious issues. I mean, she knows her stuff when it comes to putting up a building, I'll give her that. But she's not easy to work with. Not for anybody."

Jeff just listened, and Craig went on.

"She blamed my guys for her guys quitting, but it was her as much as anything else. Yeah, we were tough on them for falling behind, but that's mostly because none of them could deal with her. I hate to say it," he hesitated before finishing, "but she's kind of a hag."

Jeff didn't smile. "I'm not exactly sure what a *hag* is, Craig. Be a little more specific."

"Sorry. It's just that she makes people so mad. The way she says things. Her mannerisms. Facial expressions. Heck, even her vendors don't like dealing with her."

"Is that why you don't have her come to your meetings?"

Craig smiled, but not in a happy way. "She told you that?"

Jeff nodded.

"I didn't say she couldn't come to our meetings," Craig explained. "I said she couldn't come if she was going to piss everyone off. So she stopped showing up."

"You think she acts that way on purpose?" Jeff wondered out loud.

Craig sighed. "I don't know. But anyone who's that good at making people uncomfortable probably doesn't do it by accident."

"What about you?"

Craig was confused, but not defensive. "What do you mean?"

"What do you do that makes her mad?"

He thought about it before responding. "I don't know. I suppose I don't tolerate her attitude very well. And I should've sat down with her to rebuild the relationship when she stopped coming to the meetings."

"But you say she's good at her work from a technical standpoint?"

"Yeah." He shrugged. "She's really good at figuring out what needs to get done and keeping things organized."

"Big ego?"

Craig winced and scratched his head. "You know, as much of a pain in the ass as she is, I wouldn't say she's egotistical or self-centered. It's weird. She's just a pain, whether she knows it or not."

That phrase, *whether she knows it or not*, stuck with Jeff.

Though he was as confused as he had been a half hour earlier, Jeff felt a new sense of energy. It was that feeling he used to get when he was consulting, like a detective trying to solve a crime. *Maybe this won't be so bad after all*, he wondered. And hoped.

FINE-TOOTH COMB

When he got back to the office, Jeff found Bobby and Clare in Bobby's office. They were on a conference call, so he mouthed the words "come to my office when you're done."

They nodded, and he left in search of anything that might add to his understanding of the problems at VB.

Stopping by the large break room and grabbing a Dr. Pepper from the fridge, he found a handful of administrative employees having a late lunch at one of the large round tables. Jeff had come to know them over the course of his first months on the job, and decided to learn what he could from them.

"Mind if I sit down with you?"

They invited Jeff to join them.

Jeff opened his bottle and got right to the point. "I need to ask you a question."

The three women and two men nodded to give him permission.

"What do you guys think of the hiring situation around here?"

One of the women at the table, Kim, who served as the office receptionist and did some administrative work for Clare in HR, asked for clarification. "You mean the process?"

Jeff shrugged. "The process, the effectiveness, the overall quality. Anything."

Jeff then realized that they might be reluctant to be honest, not wanting to damage the reputations of their bosses.

"This isn't a witch hunt or anything. I'm working with Clare and Bobby to figure some things out. We want to be as open and clear as possible, so don't hold back."

Cody, a finance manager, went first. "I've been here the least amount of time of all of us, I think." He looked around the table and the others nodded to confirm his assertion. "So I probably have a better sense of the process from a new hire's perspective. And I think it was pretty good."

"What do you mean by pretty good?" Jeff asked.

"Well, everyone was friendly, and professional. It made me want to work here, for sure."

"What about the questions they asked you during interviews?"

Cody had to think about it. "It was all pretty standard. What I'd done in my career. My strengths and weaknesses."

"Anything about cultural fit? Attitude?"

Cody seemed to have a minor revelation. "Yeah, I almost forgot. A few of the interviewers wanted to know if I valued teamwork."

"What did they ask?"

Cody frowned, trying to remember. "I think they wanted to know if I was capable of being honest and vulnerable."

Kim jumped in. "I helped put the hiring binders together. The interviewers are supposed to ask about trust, and whether people are good at having healthy conflict, and a few other things."

Now Cody remembered. "Yeah, and they wanted to know if I was results-oriented. If I had a history of getting difficult things done."

Jeff was a little more impressed than he expected to be, and made a note to compliment Clare and Bobby. He'd be able to do that sooner than he thought, because at that moment the two executives walked into the break room.

"There you are," Bobby said. "We went by your office and couldn't find you."

"Sorry. I was just trying to do some research behind your backs about hiring."

The people at the table laughed, a little nervously.

"I hope you didn't throw me under the bus," Clare said to Kim.

Jeff answered for her. "Not at all. She just said that you're rarely in the office, and that they do all the work in administration."

Kim, who was spunkier than her position in the company might suggest, threw a wadded up napkin at Jeff. "That's not true."

Clare smiled and directed her question at Jeff. "So, what did you learn?"

"Well, it seems like you've done more around the teamwork stuff than posters and T-shirts."

Cody pretended to be upset. "Hey, I didn't get a teamwork poster. I was hoping for one with a picture of people rowing a boat."

Bobby added, "Or a bunch of people standing in a circle with their hands together in the middle."

Jeff could see that the sarcasm in the company went deeper than the executive level.

Clare pushed a little. "What else did you learn?"

Jeff hesitated, not wanting to say anything in front of the employees that might seem too critical. He threw caution to the wind. "Well, as much as we want to be a team company and hire team players, I don't think we know what that means. Seems like a crap shoot to me."

To prove his point, Jeff turned to Cody. "What did you say in your interview when they asked you about trust and conflict?"

He shrugged and smiled, almost in a guilty way. "Well, I guess I told them that I'm trustworthy, and that I don't mind engaging in a debate."

Jeff nodded and then asked a rhetorical question. "Do you think anyone ever says 'now that you ask, I'd have to say that I'm hard to trust, I can't admit when I'm wrong, and I have a rage problem'?"

They laughed.

"And I'm an axe murderer," Bobby added, provoking more laughter.

Clare explained, "Well, it's not just what the candidates say. It's how they say it and how they act during the interview."

Jeff didn't want to be too tough or disagreeable. "You're right, Clare. I get that. I'm just wondering if we really know what to look for. What are good indicators that the candidates are capable of the five behaviors we worked on?"

Clare nodded and shrugged simultaneously, in a way that suggested she might concede the point.

Jeff thanked the group for their time and perspectives, and then led Bobby and Clare to "Bob's office," as Jeff still called it.

PART THREE

Discovery

CLARITY

Jeff started before any of them sat down.

"I'm convinced that this teamwork thing is the key to staffing, and everything else."

Bobby responded first. "I agree. We need to get our recruiters moving right away, Clare."

"Hold on a second." Jeff sat down and put his feet on the table. "I think it's going to be a lot harder than we thought to hire eighty people." Before Clare could confirm or deny his assessment, Jeff continued. "I mean, what did we hire last year? Twenty?"

Clare corrected him. "Almost thirty."

"Right," Jeff explained, "Thirty to get twenty, because of the turnover."

Clare nodded.

Jeff directed the next question to her. "Okay, if we have to more than double that number of hires, do you think we'll be better or worse at finding the right kind of team players?"

She thought about it for a second. "Well, it wouldn't make any sense that we'd be better. I mean, more numbers, more bodies, more urgency. As much as I want to be optimistic, I think it's probably going to get a little harder."

Bobby nodded, understanding the logic.

Jeff went on. "And that means we'll probably have to hire ninety or a hundred to get sixty, right?"

They didn't want to admit it.

"Come on, guys. It's only logical."

Clare relented, sighing. "I guess that makes sense."

"Well, maybe we should just change the standards a little," Bobby proposed. "Maybe we need to be a little less picky. We probably can't afford to skip over or get rid of people who don't play well with others."

Clare shook her head. "No way. If we do that, we'll just have more of the same kind of crap that we had at Oak Ridge. And the school renovation."

Jeff frowned. "What school renovation?"

Bobby sighed and explained. "Year before last we were expanding and refurbishing a high school up in Calistoga. Sounds small, but it was actually a sizable job. Anyway, half-way through the project, we lost our best engineer because Bob wouldn't let us fire our worst engineer."

"Wait," Jeff asked. "I thought you said Bob didn't tolerate bad team players."

Clare looked at Bobby as if to say *should we tell him?* "Well, he didn't tolerate it in most employees. But sometimes when it came to the people he felt bad for, and the people he knew personally, he was kind of a wuss. He always said that he sometimes had a hard time pulling the trigger."

"How did the school situation resolve itself?" Jeff wanted to know.

Bobby answered, exasperated. "The good engineer went and started his own little firm. And I had to work my ass off to pick up the engineering slack, and that wasn't half as bad as having to work with the jackass engineer."

"And the lesson is . . . ?" Jeff asked.

Bobby rolled his eyes. "I know. I know."

"No. Say it out loud, Bobby Brady," Clare pushed him, just slightly teasing.

In a singsong voice, sounding more like a seven-year-old than the head of operations for a seventy-five-million-dollar construction firm, Bobby obeyed. "Keeping jackasses is a bad idea."

Jeff took his legs off the table and sat up in his chair. "You know, I still think that if we could just figure out how to weed out most of the jackasses, things around here would change exponentially."

"But then we'd have to hire even more people to take the places of the jackasses we get rid of," Clare reminded him.

Jeff shook his head. "I don't think so, Clare. I'd bet my job on the fact that we could get more work done with fewer people if we had real team players."

He paused and let them consider it for a few seconds.

"Think about how much easier it would be to make all the team stuff we talked about last year real. Trust, conflict, commitment, and the rest of it."

"But how are we going to do that when we have twice as much work to get done?" Bobby protested. "Teambuilding sessions aren't hotel building sessions."

"Bullshit," Jeff responded. "We're not talking about hugging or holding hands or catching each other falling off chairs. We're talking about getting people to admit when they make a mistake on a project. And to argue about the right way to get things done without worrying that they're going to offend someone. And sticking to commitments, and holding each other accountable. We need to be teaching this to everyone."

Jeff was getting excited, and continued. "Come on, Bobby. Last year when I took you guys through that teamwork project, did you think it was just a bunch of fluffy crap?"

Bobby shook his head. "No. I thought it made perfect sense."

"So what happened?" Clare asked, rhetorically.

"That's what I was going to ask you guys," Jeff added.

Clare and Bobby looked at each other.

Bobby offered an explanation. "I think we just got distracted with all the day-to-day firefighting."

Clare nodded.

Jeff went on. "I'm sure that's true. But it sounds like you also kept some key people around who didn't fit the culture." He paused for effect. "And I'm guessing that you didn't exclude them from the hiring process, either."

Suddenly, Clare's eyes went wide. "Oh crap." She looked at Bobby. "We let the jackasses hire more jackasses."

They sat there for a moment, digesting the implications of what she had said.

"I have a question." Bobby didn't wait to be called upon. "Why would a team guy like Bob be such a wuss when it comes to getting rid of people who aren't team players?"

Jeff didn't hesitate. "Because he thought he was being nice. If Bob realized how cruel it was to keep those people, he would have pulled the trigger."

"Cruel?" Bobby didn't get it.

"Yeah. Think about it." Jeff explained, "The most un-happy people in a company are the ones who don't fit the culture and are allowed to stay. They know they don't belong. Deep down inside they don't want to be there. They're miserable."

"So you're saying we should just go out and fire all the jackasses?" Clare countered. "That seems cruel, too."

Jeff shook his head. "No. You just can't go fire a bunch of people. But when you figure out who the jackasses are, you tell them that the only way they can stay, the only way they should want to stay, is if they can stop being a jackass. Or more constructively, if they can be a team player. Ninety-five percent of the time they'll do one of two things. They'll change their behavior and love you for making them do it, or they'll opt out on their own, and they'll be relieved."

"What happens if they do neither?" Bobby asked.

"Well, that's when you call Clare and a lawyer and start doing the paperwork. But trust me, it doesn't happen near as often as you think it will, as long as you don't let them off the hook for their behavior."

Bobby and Clare seemed to be generally on board with what Jeff was saying. But Clare was overwhelmed by it all.

"So where would we start?" she wanted to know.

Jeff smiled, energized by the clarity they were getting. "First, we go figure out how to recognize a real team player, the kind of person who can easily build trust, engage in healthy conflict, make real commitments, hold people accountable, and focus on the team's results. Then, we stop hiring people who can't. Finally, we help the people who are acting like jackasses change their ways or move on to different companies."

He paused, looking at a big calendar on the wall. "And we have to do all of that in the next four weeks." Then he caught himself and looked at Bobby. "I mean, month."

Bobby laughed and looked at Clare. "I'm in if you're in."

"Do we have a choice?" she replied.

Suddenly, Bobby had an epiphany. "Hey, what happens if *we're* jackasses?"

Jeff smiled. "That's a great place to start."

SELF-ASSESSMENT

Jeff decided there was no time to waste.

"Okay, I'm pretty sure you guys aren't jackasses. And I hope I'm not either. And if we are, then we're all screwed anyway."

They laughed.

"But since we're responsible for all this, let's figure out what we all have in common and what made us click with Bob. There's probably something in there that gets at the team thing."

They started looking at each other as though the answers might suddenly appear on their foreheads.

Jeff prompted them with more questions. "What made you think that this would be a good place for you to work? Think back to your interviews with Bob. How was he different or better than other people in his position that you'd met in your careers?"

Bobby went first. "Well, I know this won't help, but he definitely wasn't a jackass."

Jeff sighed. "Okay, but what was it about him that kept him out of the jackass club?"

"He didn't take himself too seriously," Clare explained. "Bob was always joking, but mostly about himself."

Bobby jumped in now. "You know, I remember the day I decided I really liked Bob. It was probably the third or fourth day on the job, and we were out at the Trinity Vineyards facility building their visitor center. Bob was great at dealing with the client, an uber-rich guy who was way too worried about whether the stones lining the entryway came from Tuscany or Calabria, or some other rich person's problem."

Bobby paused, reliving the moment in his head.

"Bob was really patient with that guy. More than I would be. But then, as soon as the guy drove off in his Range Rover, Bob started talking to the guys laying the stone and building the border wall for the flowerbeds. These weren't architects or engineers or even carpenters, but day laborers and generally unskilled workers."

For just a moment, Bobby seemed like he was getting a little emotional. "And Bob had exactly the same tone of voice and the same eye contact and the same level of interest in what they were saying as he did with the Range Rover client. And those guys noticed it, and I know they were as impressed as I was. I remember thinking, 'I wish I were like him.'"

"That's Bob," Clare confirmed, a little wistfully. "He may be the least pretentious person I know. Even slightly unsophisticated. I'm not sure what it is."

Jeff pushed on. "Would you say that you guys fit that description?"

"Not like he does," Bobby responded immediately.

"But compared to other people like yourselves," Jeff pushed. "Other executives in the industry."

Clare directed her answer at Bobby. "I think you're a lot more like Bob than you realize."

"I'm more that way now because of him."

Clare was surprised. "You weren't always that way?"

"Not really. I mean, sure, my dad would have kicked my ass if I'd been a jerk to people just because they didn't go to college or had less money than we did. But it wasn't until I came here that I really embraced that idea. Heck, at some of the places where I worked, it was bad for your career if you acted like Bob. Can you believe that?"

"You should work in the Silicon Valley," Jeff sighed. "So many people there are so concerned about being socially conscious and environmentally aware, but they don't give a second thought to how they treat the guy washing their car or cutting their grass."

"Which reminds me," Clare said, "we need to help your aunt find someone to mow the lawn at their house. Bob's been doing it himself since he bought that house. He isn't going to let go of that easily."

Jeff nodded. "I'll call Aunt Karen about that tonight. Or maybe I'll talk to Ben about it when I see him this afternoon."

Bobby was curious. "What are you talking to Ben about?"

"The same thing we're talking about now. I want to know what he looks for in team players."

"Don't you think high school basketball players and construction workers might be a little different?" Clare wondered out loud.

"Sure. But I'm guessing that they have something in common, and that Bob's son might give me an insight into how his dad thinks."

"You could just ask Bob," Bobby suggested.

Jeff disagreed. "No. First, I don't want him worrying that we need his help already. He's got plenty to think about with surgery next week. And beyond that, if Bob had a detailed grasp on what he meant by team players, we'd know by now. I think he's as unsure as we are. Or maybe just *unclear*."

They agreed. Jeff hoped Bob's son would offer a new perspective.

COACH BEN

Jeff easily spotted Ben in the back of the Starbucks, as he was a head taller than the teenagers sitting around him. He had already purchased a drink of some kind for his cousin, so Jeff wouldn't have to stand in line and try to remember whether *venti* meant medium or large.

As soon as he saw Jeff, Ben stood up and they hugged in a guy-cousins kind of way.

"Thanks for seeing me on such short notice," Jeff started. They sat down.

"Hey, I'd have coffee with you every day if I could. I'm really glad you're living up here."

"Me too. I think." Jeff laughed.

"You think?"

"No. I love it. So does Maurine. And the kids seem to like having a bigger house and a yard. But I'm just a little more concerned about work than I thought I'd be."

"Uh oh. Tell me about it."

Jeff recounted the dilemma with the hospital and the hotel and the cash flow, none of which Ben knew about.

"You really are out of the loop on the business, aren't you?" Jeff teased him.

"Hey, Dad tried to get me interested in the business. I think when he finally realized I wasn't meant for it, he stopped telling me a lot." He paused. "But I know enough to know that you definitely have a problem on your hands. And I am one hundred percent confident that my knowledge about American history, the full-court press, and fantasy football will be of absolutely no use to you."

Jeff smiled. "I don't know. There is one thing you might be able to help with. And it's big."

Ben was intrigued. "Really?"

"Yeah. We need help with teamwork."

"Are you kidding? That stuff you did for my dad last year was better than anything I've got. I've been using it with my players, teaching them how to admit when they're wrong and to hold each other accountable. I don't know what I could add."

"I'm not looking for any theories about how to make teams work. I just want to know how you identify which kids on your team are better at teamwork than others."

Ben considered the question. "I don't know. I mean, I don't have a lot of options. We're a small school and I have to make do mostly with what I have."

"But you beat teams from bigger schools all the time, right?"

"Yeah. That's because we play like a unit. No all-stars. No prima donnas. But I think that's more about the system than the kids. Like I said, I don't have a lot of players to choose from."

"But if you did, what would you look for? How do you avoid prima donnas?"

Ben sighed, again considering the question. "I don't know."

"Okay. Look at it a little differently. Imagine you were coaching at the college level. What kinds of kids would you recruit? And what kinds would you avoid?"

"I'd recruit tall ones and avoid the short ones," Ben laughed.

Jeff pushed him. "You're not serious."

"Well, no. I'm joking. I mean, I'd give my left leg for a kid over six foot five right now. But given that everyone needs size and speed and all that stuff, I'm sure there are other qualities, probably related to character, that I'd want."

"Like what?"

"Well," he was clearly thinking out loud, "probably someone who wants to be at practice. I love gym rats, but not just the kind who want to play one-on-one all day. I like the kids who come early and do extra drills. And watch film even when they don't have to." He paused before adding, "And who kind of hate to lose."

"Sore losers?"

Ben shook his head. "No, not at all. I mean, the kind who come to practice wanting to work as hard as they can to avoid losing. Coaching them is easy."

Jeff pulled out his notebook and wrote something down.

Ben was curious. "So, who else have you talked to, and what have you learned so far?"

"You're pretty much the first."

Ben's eyes widened. "Wow, I must be special."

Jeff laughed. "You are definitely special. And I knew I could count on you to buy me a five-dollar coffee."

"It's a nonfat, decaf, caramel macchiato. And I didn't buy it. I put it on the Valley Builders credit card."

"You have a company credit card?" Jeff didn't even try to hide his surprise.

Ben laughed. "No, you idiot. What do you think, Dad just gives everyone in the family carte blanche to spend the company's money? Don't you know my dad?"

Jeff was relieved. "Yes, I do. And by the way, we have to find him a gardener. He shouldn't be mowing the lawn for a while."

"Yeah, I talked to Mom about it today. My dad's not going to like that."

"Speaking of your dad, give me some insight into him."

"What do you mean?"

"Like his attitude about teamwork," Jeff suggested.

"Again, I'd think you'd know this better than me given the project you did for him. All I can say is that Dad's always said nothing is more important than teamwork, and he had this crazy intuition and usually seemed to know who had it and who didn't."

"Can you give me something from when you were growing up that gives you a sense of what he thinks makes someone a team player? Or just a good person?"

Ben laughed. "Wow. You're full of deep questions today, aren't you?" He thought about it for a few seconds. "You know, my dad coached me in different sports, and the one thing I can always remember is that he didn't have a lot of patience for kids who sucked up to him."

"What do you mean?"

"Maybe that's not the right phrase. He didn't like the kids who treated him differently than they treated one another. Or who treated the crummy players poorly."

Jeff seemed satisfied with the explanation, but Ben suddenly had a minor revelation. "Oh, and he hated when kids on his team were focused on their own stats, or on how much time they played. One time he kept one of his best ten-year-olds on the bench for an entire game because he was a ball hog and wanted to be the leading scorer on the team."

"How did the kid react? Or better yet, his parents?"

"Mom thought it was a good idea. But I was pissed."

Jeff laughed.

"But I learned my lesson."

The cousins spent the next forty-five minutes talking about family vacations and reunions from their childhood, until Ben had to leave for practice.

"Jeff, I'm really glad you're here. Dad likes to downplay things with humor, but I think you understand how much this company means to him, and to all of us."

Ben's words were heartfelt, and Jeff could tell he wasn't trying to put pressure on his cousin, even if that was the effect.

They hugged and Ben left.

Jeff stayed for another ten minutes, adding more to his notebook. As he was getting ready to leave, he found himself torn between two competing emotions—mild relief that he was making progress and disappointment that everything he was hearing seemed so obvious. He decided he needed to look harder.

FORENSICS

The next two days were filled with fighting fires and cleaning up at Oak Ridge, as well as planning for the new projects, especially the hospital. During that time, Jeff became so immersed in the business that he spent almost no mental energy thinking about teamwork and hiring, something that surprised him given the magnitude of the issue and how obsessed he seemed just forty-eight hours earlier. He was starting to get a sense of how the tangible and urgent demands of construction could crowd out more important matters. But he was determined not to let that happen to him.

So, as they were leaving a meeting with the Napa city planner, Jeff asked Clare to put together a list of all the former employees that VB had let go over the past few years and any current ones whom she had doubts about.

"I'll have it for you tomorrow morning," she assured him.

He then asked Bobby and Clare to clear their schedules for the next afternoon, something that Bobby protested but Jeff insisted on.

When they arrived at Bob's office, Jeff had written the names of all twenty-three people from Clare's list on the whiteboard.

"Let's go through these names one by one, trying to figure out any common denominators that might help us figure out what red flags we should be looking for."

As always, Bobby joked. "You mean jackass indicators?"

Clare countered. "Hey, remember that some of these employees still work here. We might want to be a little more careful about how we refer to them."

"You're going a little soft on us, Clare," Bobby teased her. "Is all that HR stuff finally getting to you?"

She laughed.

Jeff reinforced her point. "She's right, though. We need to remember that these aren't bad people. They just might not be right for a culture built around teamwork. Or maybe they've been managed by a jackass and are just doing what they think will help them get ahead."

Bobby relented. "Good point."

"How will we tell the difference?" Clare wanted to know.

Jeff had an answer. "Well, we don't need to know for sure."

Clare seemed puzzled. "What?"

Jeff explained. "Remember, once we figure out what we're looking for, then when we see someone who doesn't measure up, we just need to make it clear to them that their behavior has to change. If it does, great. It probably wasn't them after all. If it doesn't, then we know they don't belong here, and we'll help them find a better place to work."

Bobby looked at the whiteboard. "Where do we start?"

"At the top of the organization," Jeff answered confidently. "If we can deal with any questions at the highest levels, everything else will be easier."

73

Clare suddenly seemed intensely excited about the plan, and surprised both of them when she said, "Listen, you guys. We can't afford to be wussies about this. The future of this company is riding on us getting this right."

With that, Clare went to the board and circled two names. Nancy Morris, the project manager on the Oak Ridge site, and Anthony Benson, the bad engineer on the high school renovation project.

The leaders spent the next hour dissecting Nancy and Anthony, and the other two dozen or so people on the list, looking at their performance histories and behaviors. When they were finished, they had a list of predictable adjectives on the board—words like negative, lazy, insensitive, irresponsible, and self-centered. Jeff felt the same way that he did the night before.

"We must be missing something. It's too obvious," Jeff said.

"I agree," Clare confirmed. "It can't be this simple, can it?"

"If it's so simple," asked Bobby in his good natured sarcasm, "then how did we screw it up so badly?"

"Maybe we're just too close to these people," Clare wondered out loud.

Jeff shook his head. "I think we just didn't know what to look for." Then he had a suggestion. "What we need is a case study. Someone we're not so familiar with. Someone we could poke a little and test this with."

That person would present himself sooner than they could have imagined.

ADDITION BY ADDITION

Jeff took a detour on his way home from work, a twenty-minute drive that would take him by the hospital and the new site for the hotel. As the magnitude of the projects started to weigh on him, Jeff dialed Bobby's number.

"What's up, boss?" Bobby's voice came through clearly on the car's speakers.

"There's no way we can do this." Jeff was calm but confident.

"What do you mean?"

"I mean the hospital and the hotel."

"Sure we can do it. We're good at it."

"No, I don't mean the building part. I'm talking about us. You and me and Clare. We're going to need help. Imagine when these projects start heating up. We won't have time to think. We'd be challenged by the hospital alone."

The line was silent.

"Are you there? Did I drop you?"

"I'm here," he said. "I'm just thinking."

A few more seconds of silence.

Finally, Bobby weighed in. "You're right. I've had the same thoughts myself. But every time I think about bringing someone else into our group, I decide that it would be too risky. Too much trouble."

"Explain that."

"Well, Clare and I work like siblings. That's a given. Heck, we haven't even gotten used to you yet. Frankly, there's still a chance that you'll turn out to be a jackass."

Jeff laughed. "So, you're worried that we'll bring in the wrong person."

"Yeah," he hesitated. "Okay, I know this is going to sound stupid, but I just want it to be fun. I don't want to come into work and have to deal with someone I don't like to be around."

"I get that." Jeff thought about it. "But here's the thing. We're not going to like being around each other if we don't get more help."

"I know. I know. I'm in denial."

"So what are we going to do about it?" Jeff decided to let Bobby come up with a suggestion.

"We're going to tell Clare to find us the world's best, cheapest, and easiest-to-get-along-with person."

"Yeah, and before Wednesday," Jeff added.

"How about Tuesday?"

They laughed and agreed to talk about it after the weekend.

Jeff wouldn't wait that long.

SHORTCUTS

Though he generally tried not to work on weekends, Jeff decided this was a time when he needed to be making sacrifices.

"I need to set an example. In six months, everyone else will be working plenty of weekends," he explained to Maurine, who agreed with him.

As Jeff expected, Clare agreed as well, and they decided to meet at the office a little before noon.

Jeff had the same conversation with her that he had with Bobby the night before, and though Clare was even more concerned about the dynamics of the executive team, she quickly came to the conclusion that bringing someone else on at the top was unavoidable.

"So how do we go about this?" Jeff wanted to know.

"Well, I know a few recruiters who specialize in placing construction execs. We've never used them, but they could help."

Jeff was shaking his head. "That will take too long. They'll search all over the country, or at least the West Coast. And it'll take a month just to get them in here for interviews. We have to know people who know people."

Clare thought about it. "Have you asked Bobby?"

"No, he and I decided to start with you."

"I appreciate the vote of confidence," she said with just a hint of sarcasm, "but he'll have a better idea of who's available out there than I will."

"Okay, let's call him."

Two minutes later, they had Bobby on the speakerphone.

Jeff went first. "Hey, I talked to our HR lady about recruiting a new executive, and she's useless. Do you know of anyone out there who can help us?"

Bobby laughed. "Hey, are you guys having a party without me?"

"It's a party all right," Clare added. "I figured you'd know who to talk to more than me. By the way, this position we're thinking about is another VP of field ops, right?"

Jeff chimed in. "A junior Bobby."

"That's frightening," Clare exclaimed. "But sounds about right."

Within minutes, Bobby surprised himself when he came up with a short list of people who would be good sources of leads for candidates. And then he had a major revelation.

"Hey, I just thought of something. What about Ted?"

"Marchbanks?" Clare asked.

"Yeah. He could do this job in his sleep."

"I thought he retired last year?" Clare asked.

"Retired? The guy's two years older than me. He's probably bored out of his mind. And he lives over in Sonoma now."

Finally, Jeff had to ask. "Who's Ted Marchbanks?"

Clare explained. "He ran a division of North Bay Construction, a big firm located in Sausalito. He did the downtown river project about five years ago. Massive job that we didn't even bid on because it was mostly civil work having to do with the river and a few bridges, as well as a few buildings. Way too much state bureaucracy for Bob."

Bobby went on. "So he's made a pile of money and now lives near Healdsburg. I've seen him golfing a few times over here, and all he wanted to talk about was work stuff. I think he retired too early."

Clare was sold. "Let's get him in here and see if we can talk him into it."

"Is he our kind of guy?" Jeff needed to know.

"He knows what he's doing and he's available," Bobby declared.

"But what about the team stuff? Is he a jackass?"

Clare chimed in. "I have to defer to you on that one, Bobby."

"The guy is professional. Experienced. Heck, he ran a massive, complicated project for two years and they came in close to budget and on time. I don't see how he could be a jackass."

As great as all that sounded, Jeff certainly wanted to go a little deeper. "How soon do you think we can have him in here, Bobby?"

"Let me see what I can do."

Bobby wouldn't disappoint them.

TED

On Monday morning, Jeff was sitting in Bob's office responding to e-mail when Bobby came in with a big smile on his face. Jeff was surprised to see him.

"How are things at Oak Ridge?"

"Fine for now," Bobby said.

"Why are you smiling?"

"Because I have a surprise for you." He paused. "Do you have lunch plans today?"

Jeff looked down at his phone. "Yeah, I'm supposed to meet with—"

"Cancel it."

"What?"

"Cancel it. Guess who's coming here to meet us?" Before Jeff could respond, Bobby made the announcement. "Ted Marchbanks."

Jeff sat back in his chair. "How did you manage that?"

"I called my buddy down over at Chimney Rock Golf Course and he gave me Ted's number. I spoke to him last night and I was right. He's bored. Said he was intrigued."

"That is good news." Jeff smiled. "Did you tell Clare?"

"Yep. She's free. Twelve fifteen at Maria's."

"Maria's? Do you think we might want to go someplace a little more . . . good?"

"If he's a fit for our culture, he won't mind."

"You're right. I'll see you at twelve fifteen."

The restaurant was about half full, which constituted a busy day at Maria's. Jeff arrived early and asked for a booth in the back. A few minutes later, Bobby and Clare came in and found their way to the table.

"He's late. We shouldn't hire him," Jeff said with a very serious look on his face.

Bobby seemed stunned. "Wait a minute." He didn't seem to know what to say. "Maybe he's just—"

Jeff interrupted him. "I'm kidding. Sit down."

Bobby laughed. "So how long are you going to make me pay for the quitting stunt?"

"As long as you're here, my friend," he laughed. "As long as you're here."

"Okay boys. Let's focus a little." Clare sat down in a spot where she could see the door. "So what do we know about Ted?"

Bobby didn't hesitate. "He was an executive at a company that was almost four times our size. His division alone was as big as we are. He's been involved in everything from design to build to renovation, and he understands how to cut through local bureaucracies, which will be huge for the hospital project."

Jeff and Clare were clearly impressed.

"Wait a second," Bobby caught himself. "We can't hire this guy. He's going to have my job."

Clare laughed and patted Bobby on the back. "We'll always have a place for you at VB."

At that moment, the front door of the restaurant opened, letting in a blinding ray of sunlight. Out of that light stepped a man who appeared to be an angel. Then the door closed, and he became just a man again.

Wearing nice jeans and a blazer, Ted Marchbanks looked to be ten years younger than his fifty-six years. Looking around the restaurant, he spotted Bobby and headed for their table.

All three executives stood to greet him. Bobby spoke first. "It's good to see you, Ted. Thanks for meeting us on such short notice."

They shook hands.

"I was surprised and intrigued by your call yesterday, and I'm honored that you'd think of me."

He then turned to Clare. "I think I met you once before, Clare."

She seemed puzzled. "Really?"

"Didn't you attend a lunch event over in Novato a few years ago? They brought in a speaker of some kind, on leadership. You were with Bob and a few other people from your company."

"That's right," she remembered. "The North Bay Builders' Association meeting."

"If I remember correctly," he continued, "it was a snoozefest."

"Yes, it was. Some professor from an Ivy League school who didn't really connect with the construction crowd."

Ted changed the subject. "By the way, how's Bob doing?"

Clare answered, "He's at home waiting to have surgery in a couple of days. If all goes as planned, he'll be fine. But he's not coming back to work. In fact," she turned toward Jeff, "this is our new CEO, Jeff Shanley."

Jeff shook hands with Ted.

"I hear you're new to the industry, Jeff."

"That's right."

"Well, you're working with great people here," he motioned to Clare and Bobby, "so you'll have an easy time getting up to speed, I'm sure."

"I agree," Jeff replied. "And maybe you'll be able to help me, too."

Ted smiled. "Well, that's nice of you to say. I don't know that I'd have anything new to offer, but you never know."

They sat down at the table, and for the next hour and a half had a delightful and informative conversation covering everything from the industry and the job to the local economy and the nuances of building a hospital wing and a hotel.

Ted was relaxed, bright, and focused. He certainly didn't seem like someone who was ready for retirement.

Clare was curious about that. "Why did you retire, Ted?"

He hesitated. "I don't know. I guess after doing what I'd done for so long, it seemed like I should take advantage of the fact that I could afford to retire. My kids are grown. The house is paid for. My wife wanted to travel more. It just seemed like the right thing to do."

"But?" Jeff prompted him to finish the story.

Ted smiled. "Well, there's only so much golfing and antiquing and traveling you can do. I really liked the process of building things. I like the problem solving. I suppose I underestimated the benefits of the work itself."

Clare pressed him further. "Why didn't you go back to North Bay?"

He hesitated again. "As much as I enjoyed construction, that company was getting a little too big, and a little too . . .," he paused, searching for the right words, "bureaucratic. I've come to realize that it was time for a change, but maybe not retirement."

"Makes sense to me," Bobby declared.

Ted looked at his watch. "However, I am still technically retired, and if I don't make it home to help my wife clean out the garage, then boredom will be the least of my problems."

They laughed politely and thanked Ted for his time. After he left the restaurant, they stayed to debrief.

REACTIONS

s usual, Bobby went first. "Let's hire him. Now."

Neither Jeff nor Clare responded.

"Come on." Bobby pushed. "Isn't he exactly what we're looking for?"

"Probably," Jeff agreed. "He would help us in so many ways, it's crazy. His experience alone is unbelievable. And he'd have a pipeline of other people we could hire, I'm sure."

Jeff didn't sound as confident as the words should have warranted.

"So is there a problem?" Bobby asked.

"Let's just make sure he's a cultural fit," Clare explained. "How does he match up with our values?"

"Quality and safety are slam dunks," Bobby responded. "North Bay is fanatical about both."

Now Jeff weighed in. "So it all comes down to whether or not he's a team player."

"I think it's pretty obvious that he is," Bobby declared. "Did you see something I didn't?"

"I don't know," Clare shrugged. "What exactly are we looking for?"

Now Jeff was enjoying the conversation.

"Well," Bobby answered, "he's certainly not a jackass."

Clare shrugged again, a little exasperated. "So we're back to that. What exactly is a jackass?"

Bobby took a deep breath. "Well, what about those words we came up with last week? Selfish. Rude. Irresponsible. We can start there."

Jeff starting taking notes.

Clare pushed. "Okay, but what exactly do you mean by rude?"

"Come on, Clare. Rude. A jerk. Makes people uncomfortable. Says stupid and mean things. Rude."

"Give me an example of a real person who is rude. Someone we know," she asked.

Bobby only needed a second. "Okay, how about Terry Pascal?"

He looked at Jeff to explain. "He was one of our vendors. Sold us supplies. Everything from buckets and ladders to work clothes and gear."

Clare went further. "Not a bad guy. Just has no idea when he's gone too far. Overbearing. Inappropriate. Clueless."

"You said he *was* one of our vendors?" Jeff asked.

"Yeah, we told his company that we wanted someone new. The next guy was better."

Jeff had another question. "So do we have any people who fit the Terry description at VB?"

They thought about it.

"Well," Clare said, looking around to make sure that no one sitting near them could hear, "you'd have to say that Nancy falls into that category, right?"

Jeff and Bobby nodded.

Reactions

"Do you think people like Nancy and Terry do it on purpose?" Jeff asked.

"No," Clare was emphatic. "I honestly think that when it comes to dealing with people, they just," she hesitated and seemed apologetic about what she was about to say, "they're just dumb. They're not socially smart."

Jeff wrote something in his notebook and then added, "So, Ted is definitely not stupid when it comes to people. In fact, I'd say he's extremely smart."

"I think so too," Bobby declared. "That's why we should hire him."

"Hold on a second." Jeff chuckled at his excitable colleague. "That's not the only thing that makes someone a good team player."

"What are the others?" Clare wanted to know.

Jeff hesitated, flipping through his notebook. "I don't know. Everything I've written here is so obvious."

"Like what?" Bobby asked.

"I mean," Jeff shook his head. "I'm almost embarrassed to tell you guys."

Laughing, Bobby tried to take the notebook from him. "I'll just look for myself."

Jeff pulled it away. "Okay. So far, after all of our conversations and the analysis of the twenty-three people we let go or maybe should have let go, it seems to me that there are two qualities, maybe three, if we include what we just talked about."

He took his pen and wrote three phrases on the paper placemat so that everyone could see them: *ego, hard work,* and *people.*

"They have to do with having no ego, working really hard, and knowing how to deal with people."

Clare frowned. "Don't use the word *ego*. Find a positive word."

Jeff was puzzled, then saw the problem. "Oh, right." He scratched out *ego* and wrote *unpretentious* in its place."

The three teammates sat looking at the words Jeff had written. If it had been a cartoon, smoke would have been coming out of their ears because they were studying the words so intently.

"Again, this seems too simple," Jeff apologized.

Clare jumped in. "No, I think we may be on to something here, even if it's obvious. Let's go back to our list of difficult people and see if it explains their issues."

As they started to think about the question, Jeff looked down at his watch. "Oh crap. It's almost two-thirty." He looked at Bobby. "You and I have a meeting with the hospital architects."

"Let's pick up this conversation tomorrow," Clare proposed.

They agreed, and Jeff and Bobby asked Clare to pay the bill so they could go.

PART FOUR

Implementation

JUGGLING

Things at the Oak Ridge site were crazy the next day, more than Bobby had expected.

"Nothing major," Bobby explained, "but if I don't spend the next few days with the inspectors there, we could be in a little trouble."

So Clare and Jeff agreed to move Ted's formal follow-up interview to later in the week, giving them more time to settle on their definition of a team player.

The next day was Bob's surgery, and while the office continued to be busy, plenty of people were worrying, praying, and checking in with the Shanley family for updates. When news came that the procedure had been successful and that Bob's prognosis was a good one, there was great relief in the VB office. Unfortunately for the leaders of the firm, that relief was short lived because their anxiety merely shifted to the future of the business.

The following day would be Ted's interview, and Jeff decided he needed to meet with his two lieutenants immediately to resume their discussion about getting greater clarity about what a jackass was, and what it meant to be a team player, so they could be prepared for the interview. They agreed to bring food into the office and stay as late as was necessary.

By six-thirty, Indian food had been set out on Bob's desk, and Clare and Jeff were waiting for Bobby to arrive.

"I don't remember exactly where we landed the other day when Bobby and I had to leave," Jeff admitted.

Clare reminded him. "We were going to take the words you wrote on the placemat and test them against some of our difficult people."

At that moment, Bobby entered. "You mean jackasses."

Clare rolled her eyes playfully.

"Right," Jeff remembered. "Did you remember to grab the placemat?"

Clare was already holding up the salsa-stained remnant in her hands.

Bobby went straight for the food but kept the conversation going. "I've got another employee for us to analyze: Tommy Burleson."

Clare winced. "Oh, I'd almost forgotten about him."

"Was he a jackass?" Jeff asked.

Clare looked at Bobby. "What do you think?"

He thought about it. "I don't know. He wasn't a jerk, that's for sure. Which is probably why we kept him here for two years before we asked him to leave. But he certainly wasn't a good guy to have on your team."

"Why not?" Jeff asked.

"Tommy was one of the most frustrating people I've ever had to deal with," Clare announced. "The guy was funny. Charming. Bright."

"Sounds like a nightmare," Jeff commented sarcastically.

"That's the thing," Clare said. "As wonderful a guy as he was, we just couldn't get him to step up."

"You mean he wasn't hardworking? He was lazy?"

Bobby smiled and winced at the same time. "That's what was so hard about Tommy. You wouldn't say he was your classic lazy person. He would do what you asked him to do."

Clare finished, "And nothing else."

Bobby agreed. "He'd do just enough to stay out of trouble, but he'd never really tackle a project or a problem with a sense of urgency. Or passion."

Clare added, "It would have been a lot easier if he were a jerk. Or a sloth. But he wasn't."

"So he was lacking passion?" Jeff prodded, seeking closure around the right word.

Bobby winced again. "No. Tommy definitely had passion, just not about work. He was totally into the company softball team and fly fishing and the Civil War."

Clare tried to capture it. "He just wasn't hungry."

Jeff wrote something in his notebook and then asked Clare, "What do you mean by that?"

"I mean, he wasn't the kind of guy who had a sense of personal motivation or a desire to do something big." She paused to think about it. "Maybe it's because he came from a pretty comfortable background and just didn't have anything to prove. Or to accomplish. I don't know."

Bobby's mouthful of chicken tikka masala didn't stop him from talking. "He's the kind of guy who would be the best next-door neighbor in the world, but not someone you'd want to depend on. Or go into business with."

Jeff was nodding and looking at his notebook. "Hungry. I like that."

"So do I," said Clare. "That's better than hardworking." She turned toward Bobby. "Speaking of hungry, are you going to wait for us to say grace before you inhale all of the naan?"

Bobby apologized and they bowed their heads.

A few minutes later, after everyone had filled their plates, Jeff went to the whiteboard and found a corner where there were no names. He wrote *hungry*.

"Okay," he announced, "I think that's the right word. We need to hire people who are hungry. They go beyond what is required. Passionate about the work they're doing. Hungry."

They all nodded, and Jeff continued. "And then there was the other concept we talked about after Ted left yesterday."

Clare nodded, holding up the placemat. "People. It had to do with being smart about people."

Jeff wrote *smart* on the board. "Right. And Ted is really smart."

"That doesn't sound right," Bobby objected. "It sounds like you mean intelligent."

"I think that's why I like it," Clare said. "It's not your typical 'nice guy' description. It's like emotional intelligence, but simpler. It just means a person has to know how to act and what to say and what not to say. People smart. Which is a lot more than being nice."

"And I think calling it smart will make people think about it in a different way," Jeff agreed. "They won't write it off as something soft or easy."

Bobby wasn't sold. "But you can't be a jackass if you're smart about people. This sounds like it should be the only thing that matters."

Jeff thought about it and pushed back. "I disagree. A smart person could be a jackass. In fact, that would be the worst kind of jackass."

"Explain that," Clare asked.

"Well, you could be really good about knowing what to say and how to say it and how to charm everyone you deal with," Jeff said. "But if deep down inside you were doing it for yourself, for your own ambitions, that would make you a duplicitous jackass."

"Use words I can spell, smart man," Bobby joked.

Jeff smiled. "Two-faced. Deceitful. Dishonest."

A light seemed to go on above Clare's head. "Maybe that's where the next idea comes into play."

"What idea?" Bobby asked.

Clare looked at the placemat. "Well, the word you wrote here was *unpretentious*."

Jeff nodded. "Right. That came from our discussion about Bob. People at VB don't fit in if they're pretentious."

"I think pretentiousness isn't the right concept." Surprisingly, it was Bobby who was pushing on this one. "Or maybe I'm wrong. I mean, pretentious people are definitely jackasses, but there's more to it than that. What makes someone stand out here, in a bad way, is when they're . . . arrogant." He seemed confident that was the right word. "What's the opposite of arrogance?"

"Humility," Clare responded enthusiastically. "Jackasses aren't humble."

"That's it," Bobby said. "And that's Bob for sure."

Jeff drew three circles on the board, creating a Venn diagram of sorts. He then wrote the words *humble, hungry,* and *smart* next to the circles.

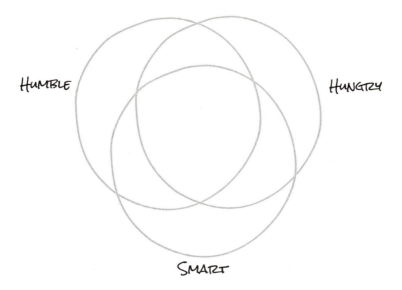

HUMBLE   HUNGRY

SMART

He went back to his plate of food, and the three executives ate as they studied the diagram.

For the next hour, they chose employee after employee, some who were difficult, others who were all-stars, and others who fell somewhere in between. They evaluated them against the three new words, placing them in the circles where they belonged.

Every all-star easily met a pretty high standard for being humble, hungry, and smart, and they were placed in the middle segment. Some barely failed to meet the standard in just one area and were close to the middle of the chart, while others struggled with more than one of the qualities and were further out from the middle.

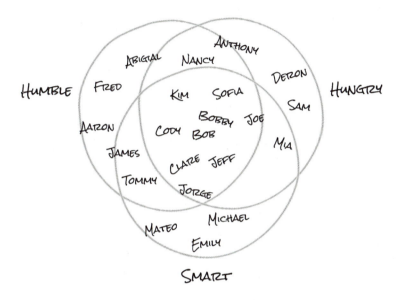

Jeff insisted that the leadership team be evaluated the same way, and though each person made it into the middle segment, what was interesting is that they landed in different locations.

By the time the food was mostly gone and they had placed almost two dozen names somewhere in the diagram on the whiteboard, Clare and Bobby were convinced they were on to something.

But Jeff was still uncertain. "It still sounds too simple to me." He kept looking at the three words. "And yet, I don't see anything missing. I guess it's just the combination of the three."

"That's it," Clare announced, walking to the whiteboard and circling the middle segment in bright red. "The magic here is just that if even one of the qualities is missing in a big way, you've got yourself a jackass."

Bobby laughed. "Hell, I could have told you that."

Clare threw her pen at Bobby.

They decided they should start using the model right away in the hiring process, which Bobby suggested they call the "no jackass test." The first of those tests would be the next morning with Ted Marchbanks.

TED AGAIN

The day was set up as a comprehensive interview session for Ted. A few people from the field and Clare would be meeting with him individually during the morning, followed by a one-on-one lunch meeting with Jeff. He made it clear that the primary goal would be to discern whether Ted was humble and hungry, having already determined that he was smart.

Ted's first interview would be with Craig, the foreman from the Oak Ridge project, so Jeff arranged to meet Craig an hour early to help him understand how he might go about evaluating Ted for the two desired virtues. Jeff conceded that this might be difficult, since he didn't really have great working definitions for what those words meant from an observable, behavioral point of view.

Jeff's instructions for Craig were simple. "Just try to get a sense for whether he wants to keep working hard, whether he still has the desire to commit himself to the job, or whether this is simply a distraction from his retirement boredom."

Craig wrote that down. "I get it. What about humble?"

"Well, use your judgment. You know what someone looks like who isn't humble, right?"

Craig smiled. "Bobby would probably call him a jackass."

Jeff laughed. "Bobby is remarkably consistent in his language, isn't he?"

Craig asked Jeff another question. "So what kinds of things would *you* look for, in terms of humility?"

Jeff didn't hesitate. "Like I said, I think it's more about looking for indications that he's not humble. Arrogance. Condescension. Dismissiveness. Self-centeredness."

Craig made a few notes. "Makes sense. So, do you want me to come see you tomorrow to tell you what I think?"

Jeff's eyes went wide. "No way. I want to hear from you as soon as you're done."

Craig seemed a little surprised, so Jeff explained. "I need to know what you learned, so I can figure out what to look for in my lunch interview. And I might even give the other morning interviewers some of your insights to help them drill down harder in the right areas."

"Wow." Craig was impressed. "You're not messing around."

Jeff smiled. "Can't afford to mess around. Too much on the line here."

Craig frowned. "I don't want to be pushy here, Jeff." He hesitated.

"What? Ask me anything."

"You said there's too much on the line. Is there something I don't know about?"

Jeff hesitated for a second, considering how much to tell Craig. "Okay. Here's the thing. We've got so much work coming up, and we need to do a crap load of hiring."

Craig nodded, unsurprised.

"Which means we have to find people who aren't going to create problems out in the field."

Craig smiled and shook his head. "I know something about that."

"Exactly. Imagine what will happen if we keep having problems like that next year."

Craig seemed to get it. "Oak Ridge is killing me. I don't think I'd make it if things got worse."

Jeff smiled, but not in a joyful way. "Exactly. And if this guy, Ted, isn't all about teamwork, if he doesn't eat, sleep, and breathe humility and hunger, there is no way all the people working for him will. And he won't hire those kinds of people either."

Craig started thumbing through his notes. "So, let's go over this again. I need to ask—"

Jeff interrupted him, almost laughing. "Relax, you don't have to figure it all out yourself. Other people are going to be meeting with him, too. Just go over what we talked about and let me know what you think when you're done."

"Got it." Craig seemed relieved.

At that moment, Kim, the receptionist and HR assistant, came into the office. "Excuse me. Ted Marchbanks is waiting."

DEBRIEF

After Craig had finished his half-hour conversation with Ted, Jeff asked Kim to take Ted to his next interview, and he had Craig stay to debrief. As soon as Ted and Kim were gone, he dove in.

"So what do you think?" Jeff shut the door.

"I think he's a great guy," Craig answered without hesitating. "And he knows the business cold."

"Do you think he's hungry?"

Craig thought about it. "Yeah, I mean, he definitely wants the job. And he wants to be busy again."

"Does he seem like he has a strong work ethic?"

"I don't know how you come to run a division of NBC if you aren't a hard worker."

"NBC?"

"Yeah, North Bay Construction."

Jeff laughed. "Right."

Craig was curious. "Do you have reasons to believe he isn't hungry?"

"No. I just have to make sure that he really fits." Jeff looked through his notebook. "How about the passion? Is he still passionate about construction and the idea of doing great work?"

Craig thought about it for a second, and started nodding. "Yeah. He talked about the new wing of the hospital, and said that he likes doing that kind of work. He certainly doesn't seem like the kind of guy who should be retired."

Jeff made a note. "What about humility? Was he condescending or disrespectful in any way? Is he down-to-earth?"

"Down-to-earth? I don't know. He wasn't condescending to me or disrespectful. As far as ego goes, I only spent a half hour with him, but I didn't see any red flags." He thought about it all for a moment. "I'd say he's a pretty good guy. Based on my experience during the last half hour, I'd probably work for him."

Jeff made a few more notes. "Okay. Thanks, Craig."

They shook hands, and as Craig was leaving the office, Jeff stopped him.

"Hey, how are things with Nancy going?"

Craig didn't hesitate. "Better. She's still a mystery to me. But I convinced her to come to my meetings again. And I've coached my guys not to get too pushed out of shape when she says something that might piss them off."

Jeff was relieved. "Good for you." He paused before asking the next question. "Just between you and me, do you think she's humble?"

Craig seemed surprised by the comment. "I don't know that I'd use that word to describe her."

"Okay," Jeff continued. "But is she arrogant? Does she think she's better than everyone else?"

103

He shook his head. "That's not how I'd describe her either. She treats everyone the same, pretty much. And doesn't complain about having to do grunt work. She's just a," he hesitated, "well, like I said, she's a puzzle."

Jeff appreciated that he didn't use the word *hag*.

DIGGING

Jeff went to Clare and prepped her for the conversation she would be having with Ted in ten minutes.

"I certainly don't think he's lazy or dispassionate," Jeff explained. "So there aren't any questions about hunger."

Clare completed the thought. "And he knows how to read people and get them to like him, so he's definitely smart enough. Which means that humility is the only question, and it sounds like he hasn't done anything to make us think—"

Jeff interrupted her. "No, he hasn't. But he hasn't done anything to make me think he is humble, either."

Clare frowned. "What would that look like?"

"I don't know. In fact, I'm not exactly sure what humility is."

Clare smiled. "Well, that might be a small problem."

Jeff agreed. "I know. It's just that humility is a tricky thing. How do you know if a person is just really smart and knows how to present himself like he's humble? It's not just about avoiding being an overtly arrogant person. I mean, how many people brag about themselves all the time and are openly condescending to others?"

"I know a few," Clare said.

"So do I," said Jeff, "but most of them aren't interviewing for jobs like this." He thought about it for a second. "Or better yet, most of them wouldn't make it past the first ten minutes of an interview. They're easy to spot."

Clare agreed. "Yeah, the subtle ones are the most dangerous."

"Which is why we need to be really, really careful— almost paranoid—about this when we're hiring someone so senior in the company."

Clare closed her door. "So, it sounds like you're having doubts about Ted then."

Jeff shook his head. "I don't know if it's doubt. But I don't have anything close to confirmation yet that he's our guy."

"You mean, that he's humble."

"Yeah. That's my only question," Jeff confirmed.

At that moment there was a knock on the door, and Kim popped her head in.

"Should I send Ted in?"

Clare took a breath. "No, I'll come get him." She looked at Jeff and smiled. "I have an idea. Let's see what I can figure out."

NAMES

lare decided that the best way to get an accurate read on Ted might be to take him out of the office and put him in a less structured environment.

"I've got an errand to run, and I thought we could do our interview while we're out," Clare announced.

Ted shrugged. "Sounds fine to me."

They got into Clare's minivan, with Cheerios dotting the floor, and headed for Target. "I have to get a birthday present for one of my daughters' friends," Clare explained.

During the drive, they talked about Ted's management philosophy and about the people he managed at NBC. Most of his answers were certainly appropriate, though not specific. According to Ted, he hadn't had any real problems with subordinates.

As for the nontraditional setting of the interview, Ted handled it all just fine.

On the way back to the office, they crossed over one of the new bridges that spanned the Napa River, and Ted announced excitedly, "This was one of my projects." They talked about the long hours he had worked and the relationships with state and city politicians that he had to maintain.

When they returned to the VB parking lot, Clare dropped Ted off at the front door so he wouldn't be late for his next interview. "Check in with Kim and she'll show you where to go."

"Which one is Kim?" he asked politely.

Though she was a little surprised, Clare didn't think much of the question at the time. "She's the receptionist who took you to your interviews this morning. She works for me."

After she dropped Ted off, she went to Jeff's office and shared her thoughts with her boss. She was as convinced as ever that Ted was as smart as any executive she had ever met and that he was hungry. And as for his humility, like Craig, she saw no glaring red flags. "The guy's a diplomat. Unflappable. I can't imagine why we wouldn't hire him."

Jeff frowned. "What's wrong?"

"What?" she asked.

"The way you said that. 'I can't imagine why we wouldn't hire him.' You sound like you're not convinced."

Clare thought about it, looking out the window. "Well, maybe I'm not. I don't know what it is."

"How do you feel about him being part of our leadership team? You and me and Bobby and him?"

"That's the thing. I can't tell if it's the idea of adding a new face to the team that bothers me, or if there's something specific about Ted."

At that moment, Kim knocked on the door and looked in. "Sorry to bother you guys. I just want to make sure that we're clear on the rest of the day." She looked at Jeff. "After the next interview, you're taking Ted to lunch, right?"

Clare confirmed for Jeff. "Yes. Where do you have them eating?"

"I thought Pacific Blues in Yountville would be good. They have the best mac and cheese in the Valley."

"Never been there," Jeff admitted, "but sounds good to me."

As Kim was backing out of the doorway, Jeff stopped her.

"Hey, can I ask you a question, Kim?"

"Depends on what it is," she teased him.

"Fair enough. So what do you think of Ted?"

Kim wasn't prepared for the question. "What do you mean?"

Jeff smiled. "I mean, what do you think of him? Would you hire him? Would you want to work with him every day?"

Kim seemed a little uncomfortable. "Wow. That's tricky."

Clare was curious. "Why is it tricky?"

Kim came into the office and shut the door. "Because if I tell you he hit on me and then you hire him, he's not going to like that."

"Did he hit on you?!" Clare demanded to know.

Kim laughed. "No. It's just an example. What I mean is that I wouldn't want to say something bad about someone who I might have to work with. Or for."

Jeff sat up in his chair. "Well, first of all, you're a big part of this place, Kim. I'd trust your opinions as much as anyone else's. Hell, I should have put you on the interview schedule."

Kim laughed.

Clare went next. "Do you have something bad to say about Ted?"

"I don't know. I mean, I've met people that were a lot worse."

"In what way?" Jeff asked.

"Well, I can tell you that he wasn't exactly gregarious when he arrived this morning."

"How so?" Clare seemed surprised.

"Well, he was in the lobby for fifteen minutes, just me and him, and he didn't ask me a single question. Or even notice that I was there. And I've been taking him around for the past few hours, and I don't think he's said a word to me other than 'where's the bathroom?' or 'can you charge my phone?'"

Clare looked at Jeff to see what he was thinking. He was taking notes.

"Did he thank you," Jeff asked, "for charging his phone?"

Kim had to think about it. "Probably. I don't really remember."

"Then he definitely wasn't effusive about it."

Kim shook her head. "No. I got the sense that he thought it was my job." She frowned. "I'm not saying he's a jerk. Not at all. But if he ran into me on the street tomorrow, I'd be surprised if he'd remember me at all."

And that's when it hit Clare. "He didn't know your name!"

"What?" Kim was confused.

"When I dropped him off ten minutes ago, I told him to find you, and he asked who Kim was."

"Are you sure?" Jeff asked.

Clare nodded. "Yeah. I think it was pretty clear."

Suddenly Kim felt bad. "Listen, I don't want to torpedo this guy. Maybe he was distracted or was having a bad morning."

Jeff was measured. "You're right, Kim. And you're not torpedoing Ted. We're not going to jump to conclusions here. But we have to be prudent about this, and we also have to be thorough."

Clare was just about to thank Kim and ask her to leave when something occurred to her. "You know what we should do?" It was a rhetorical question, directed at no one in particular, so she answered it herself. "We should find out if this is just a bad day, an anomaly, or if it's typical for Ted."

"How do you suggest we do that?" Kim wanted to know.

"Well, when we do a reference check at NBC, let's have a few informal discussions with the administrative staff there."

Jeff was confused. "Are we just going to call the front desk and ask, 'excuse me, is Ted Marchbanks a jerk?'"

Kim laughed. "Actually, it wouldn't be that hard. If he is, they'll be glad to tell me. If not, they'll be glad to tell me. I'll have an answer for you in fifteen minutes."

Suddenly Clare and Jeff were laughing like fifteen-year-olds planning to take their parents' car on a joyride.

"We can't do this, can we?" Jeff looked to Clare for guidance.

She replied, but without much conviction. "Well, not formally. I mean, that would be unprofessional."

Kim countered, "But it wouldn't be as unprofessional as not finding out."

"I agree," Jeff weighed in.

Kim went on. "I mean, if that's how he treats people below him on the food chain, then I wouldn't want him here. That's not VB at all."

Clare and Jeff looked at each other as if to say *she's right*.

"So how do we get that information the right way?" Clare wondered.

111

Kim responded in a serious tone. "My brother can hack into their personnel records and see if he has any complaints filed against him."

Clare was appalled. "Tell me you're kidding."

"No, he's really good at stuff like that."

Jeff squinted at the receptionist in disbelief.

Clare began to scold her employee. "But Kim, that's—"

Kim interrupted her boss. "Come on, you guys. I'm joking. I'm not an idiot."

Clare and Jeff broke into laughter.

"But I do have a brother, and his girlfriend's sister used to work there. I can see if she'll talk to us. There's certainly nothing wrong with that."

Jeff brought the conversation to a close. "That would be great. Make sure you do it in an appropriate, respectful way. And I'll see what I can learn this afternoon in my discussion with him."

"What are you going to do? Ask him if he treats his admin staff poorly?" Clare wondered out loud.

Jeff shrugged. "Maybe."

NAKED

Jeff and Ted drove separately to Yountville for lunch, as the restaurant was in the same direction that Ted would be headed afterward. Pacific Blues wasn't terribly crowded, which allowed Jeff to find a good spot with empty tables around them.

After they ordered, Jeff dove in.

"How have the interviews gone so far?" he asked.

"Fine. Everyone's been very nice. I've always known that VB was a place full of good people."

Jeff decided to be as direct as possible. "Do you feel like the culture here would be a good fit for you?"

"Sure," Ted responded without really thinking. "Like I said, this is a good company."

Jeff pushed a little. "How would you describe the culture at North Bay? And how do you think this one will be different?"

Ted raised his eyebrows, as though he hadn't thought about it. "Well, I guess you guys are a lot smaller, so it might be a little less formal."

"North Bay was formal?"

"Yeah, I'd say so. I mean, more suits and ties and fancier offices."

"Was that a good fit for you?"

Ted shrugged. "I can roll with just about anything. And I did enjoy it there."

"What about the people who worked for you there? How would they describe your management style?"

Ted shifted in his chair and responded confidently. "They'd say I was a good boss. Demanding, but I took care of my people."

"What do you mean by that?" Jeff asked casually.

"Well," Ted had to think about it, "I made sure they were well paid and that they had good opportunities for growth in the company when they finished my projects."

"What about people who didn't work on one of your projects? Corporate staff. Admin. If I asked them about you, what would they say?"

Ted now had a puzzled look on his face. With nothing more than a hint of annoyance, he responded, "I never had any problems with people, if that's what you mean."

Jeff could sense the discomfort in the moment and decided to throw caution to the wind. "I'm sorry if this seems cryptic, Ted. Let me be more transparent here." He took a breath. "Being intentional about the culture is really important to us. More than ever now that Bob is gone. And one of the biggest things we value is how people treat one another."

Ted nodded as though he admired that.

"And the thing about Bob is that he treated everyone the same. It didn't matter what your job was or what department you worked in, or how much money you made."

"I think that's a good thing," Ted responded diplomatically. "Bob is a good guy, and I'd say I agree with all that."

Jeff was frustrated that he wasn't communicating the importance of humility in a way that sounded more than generic. He decided to be a little more blunt.

"See, we've decided that we're going to be kind of fanatical about that." He paused and went one step further, "In fact, I'm going to make it so important that a person who didn't share that attitude would kind of hate working here. It would be really unpleasant for them."

Though Ted certainly didn't respond with any sense of shock, Jeff was sure that he flinched just a little when he heard the word *unpleasant*.

But even if he did, Ted recovered immediately. "I think having a strong culture is very important. In fact, that's probably an area in which NBC could have been a little better."

Jeff nodded, considering Ted's comment. Then he decided to go for broke. "Ted, our culture is all about being humble, hungry, and smart in how we interact with each other. We think that's what creates an environment for teamwork." Jeff was being more confident than he had expected, but decided that subtlety was not going to work. "And we're going to eat, drink, and sleep those things. We're going to talk about them in recruiting, interviews, company meetings, performance reviews, compensation decisions, everything."

"What about performance?" Ted asked, a little skeptically. "Delivering projects on time and within budget?"

Jeff thought about it. "Those are critical. No doubt. But I believe those will be the outcomes we'll get if we bring humble, hungry, and smart people together and give them clarity about what needs to be done."

Ted nodded, but didn't seem convinced. "Sounds like a good plan to me. I think I could help with all that."

Jeff backed off a little, spending the next twenty minutes asking Ted how he would go about sharing resources across the two new projects and how he'd handle hiring. It was an education, and Jeff came to appreciate Ted's expertise and even enjoy him as a person. But he still wasn't convinced he was right for VB.

When time was up for the interview, he asked one final question. "Who can I talk to at NBC about your time there and your fit for our culture?"

Ted hesitated. "Well, some of my people have moved on, and I'd need to check with—"

Jeff interrupted him, politely. "That's okay. It could be anyone, even if they're not there anymore. Just people who know you well and would have the best insights."

Ted paused, and seemed a little off balance. "Let me send you a few names this afternoon, if that's okay."

Jeff assured him that it was, and they ended the interview.

"Ted, you're a remarkably talented person, and if VB is the right place for you, then you'll be a great asset here."

As they shook hands, Jeff was certain that Ted was struggling to decide whether to be flattered or threatened.

POINTS OF REFERENCE

Toward the end of the day, Jeff checked his texts and e-mail; Ted had yet to send him references. Clare stopped by, hoping to start the process.

"Nothing yet," he announced, to her disappointment.

Clare tried to be resourceful. "Well, I know a client of Ted's from a few years ago. I can try him. And maybe Kim's brother's sister's second cousin twice removed will give us something soon."

Jeff laughed. "I hate waiting, too."

Clare made a sudden decision. "Oh, what the hell. Let's just call the head of HR over at NBC. I've met her a few times. Ted's not working there anymore, so maybe she'll help us out."

She went right to the phone.

"So what we're after here is just humility?" she asked while scrolling through her contacts. "We're not going to cover anything else?"

Jeff shrugged. "I don't know. I mean, if we don't have doubts about his technical competence, I think we ought to focus on the one thing we're concerned about."

"I'm just so used to doing generic reference checks," Clare remarked just as she found the number. "It's going to be odd drilling down on one thing."

"Good," Jeff smiled. "We must be doing something right. After all, we want VB to be an odd company, in a good kind of way."

"What do you mean?"

"Well, people who don't fit should think we're a little strange, right?"

Clare winced. "Strange? I don't think it's strange to be humble and hungry and smart."

"Not for us. But if someone were socially clueless, they'd think we were silly for caring so much about being smart."

She began nodding her head.

"And if a person had a big ego, they'd think this was a strange place to work."

Now Clare seemed relieved. "I guess you're right. Strange in a good way."

"Absolutely. Let's find out if Ted Marchbanks is strange in a good way."

Clare hit the speakerphone and dialed the number, whispering to Jeff, "her name is Marie."

A woman answered after the first ring. "This is Marie."

"Marie, this is Clare Massick, the head of HR at Valley Builders, and I've got Jeff Shanley with me, our CEO. I don't know if you remember me, but we've met a few times."

"Sure I remember you," Marie said matter-of-factly. "What can I do for you guys?"

"Well, I was hoping you could tell us something about Ted Marchbanks. We've been talking to him about a job here, and we wanted to get a sense from you about whether you think he'd be a good fit for us."

Marie hesitated. "Well, Ted is very competent and professional."

"Great," Clare responded. "What about his attitude? Would you say he's open to feedback and willing to admit when he's wrong?"

The line was silent for a moment, until Marie finally responded. "Like I said, Ted is like most of the people here. He's professional, positive, and hardworking."

Clare frowned at Jeff, as if to say *that's a lame answer.*

Jeff followed up. "Can you tell us why Ted left NBC?"

Marie answered immediately. "No, I'm afraid I can't. That's against our policy. But I can say that he wasn't terminated for cause, and that we would recommend him to a potential employer."

Clare hit the mute button and said to Jeff, "How would they know if he would be a good fit for that employer?"

Hitting the mute button again, Clare tried once more. "Marie, what do you think administrative people who worked for Ted would say about him?"

Marie answered immediately. "We never had any formal complaints about him. I don't know what else to tell you."

It was clear that this woman wanted off the phone and wasn't going to be a fountain of useful information.

Clare brought the conversation to a close. "Thanks, Marie. We appreciate your time."

"Sure. Good luck in your hiring," she responded cordially, and ended the call.

"Well, that was worthless," Jeff complained.

"Yes, it was. But that's what you get these days when you call a company that just wants to avoid getting sued."

"Well, hopefully we'll get his references before tomorrow morning so we can get something real." Clare paused. "What's your gut telling you?"

Jeff frowned. "I'm fifty-fifty. Maybe a little higher than that. I just hope we get something that tells us one way or the other from one of these references, or from Kim's brother's girlfriend's cousin's best friend."

Clare laughed, just as Jeff's cell phone rang.

"I'll let you take that. I've got a meeting." Had she known who was calling, she would have stayed.

THE CALL

Jeff didn't recognize the number. He had never talked to Ted on the phone.

"This is Jeff."

"Jeff, it's Ted Marchbanks."

"Hey, Ted. I was just checking to see if you'd sent me your references yet. What's up?"

"Well, about that. After lunch today, I sat down and talked to my wife. And," he stammered, "well, I'm thinking that maybe I shouldn't be diving back into work so quickly."

Jeff was stunned. "Wow. Tell me more about that."

"It's just that maybe I'm being a little impulsive," Ted said, impassively. "I don't know if I'm ready to walk away from retirement just yet."

Jeff didn't believe a word that he was hearing. It all sounded like an excuse to him. He was stunned.

"I have to tell you, I'm a little surprised," Jeff said. "Or maybe more than a little."

"I know. I'm sorry if I led you guys on."

Jeff responded reflexively. "No, no. I mean, it's been just a few days. And you have to do what's best for you and your wife. Don't worry about that."

After a slightly awkward pause, Jeff confirmed, "So, you're saying that you're definitely pulling out of the process then?"

Another pause. "Yeah," Ted responded, "I'm out of the process."

"All right. Well, stay in touch with us. If you change your mind, let us know." Jeff hoped that didn't sound like Ted had a job waiting for him if he wanted it.

"Thanks, Jeff. Good luck to you guys."

And that's how it ended.

Jeff sat at his desk sorting through a variety of emotions, most of which were not pleasant.

On the one hand, he dreaded having to tell Clare, and especially Bobby, that the man they had hoped would solve a big part of their problem was gone. That would be a serious morale bust for them.

Beyond that, he didn't know that there was anyone else out there whom they'd be able to find on relatively short notice. The logistics of that alone were enough to drive Jeff into a mild funk.

But he was also feeling a bizarre sense of relief, one that he hoped he'd be able to describe to Bobby and Clare. At this point, he wasn't sure they'd be buying it.

ANGST

Before Jeff could go find Clare, she called to announce that her meeting had been cancelled and that Bobby was on his way back to the office.

"He wants an update on the Ted situation," she explained. "I told him that there was no news yet."

Jeff tried to hide any sense of disappointment in his voice. "Why don't you guys come by anyway," he suggested.

Fifteen minutes later, the two executives were walking through Jeff's door, smiling, with no idea what they were about to learn.

"Hey boss," Bobby announced, before adjusting his approach. "Uh oh. What's wrong?"

"Does something seem wrong?" Jeff asked.

"You seem kind of down," Clare confirmed. "What's up?"

Jeff took a breath. "Sit down."

"Uh oh," Bobby repeated.

"Okay, here's the thing. Ted just called and," Jeff paused, "he opted out of the interview process."

"What?" Bobby asked first. "Why?"

"He said he's not sure he wants to come out of retirement after all."

Bobby was suddenly very serious. "Bullshit. That guy hated retirement. What did he say?"

Jeff looked at Clare before answering. "That's what he said. But I think there was more."

"More what?" Bobby wanted to know.

Clare jumped in and directed her question at Jeff. "Do you think we might have scared him off?"

"What?" Bobby seemed almost angry. "How?"

"I think he might have felt a little threatened by all the cultural questions," Jeff admitted. "Either he was offended, or didn't like what he was hearing."

Bobby was incredulous. "Have we heard anything from his references?"

"He never sent us references," Jeff explained. "But we did reach out to a few contacts that we thought might help us."

Clare added, "We called the head of HR from NBC, but she gave us nothing, just a generic acknowledgment that he wasn't fired. The others haven't called back yet."

No one spoke for a few long seconds.

"Do you guys think we might be taking this culture stuff too far?" Bobby wasn't really asking a question. "I mean, we're screwed."

Jeff wanted to argue with Bobby but decided to let him vent as much as he needed to. He wasn't finished.

"No one is perfect. We can't afford to put all these restrictions on the people we hire." He turned to Jeff. "You said yourself that we'll have to hire even more people if we want to hit our new numbers, and then you go and make it harder. That's like tying one hand behind your back in a boxing match. This is crazy."

Clare countered, "Bobby, this isn't just an employee. It's a leader, someone who will be hiring other people. He's a guy we're going to have to work with and depend on. And if he's not right, there's no way we can expect others to get it."

Jeff was glad that Clare seemed to understand. Until she turned to him.

"So is there any way we can get him to reconsider? Did he seem like he was sure of the decision?"

"I don't think he's going to reconsider," Jeff answered. "And I'm not convinced we want him to."

Bobby sighed. "Maybe the humble, hungry, smart thing is wrong."

Clare shrugged.

Jeff couldn't believe that one man's decision not to take a job could lead intelligent people to abandon their standards and principles so easily. As badly as he wanted to do something to prove that their work around humble, hungry, and smart was right, he didn't see an opportunity at that moment. He just sat there for a few awkward seconds.

Bobby broke the silence. "I've got to be over at Oak Ridge in ten minutes. Then I have a dinner thing. I'll see you guys tomorrow." Then he added, without looking Jeff in the eye, "I'm sorry I got so upset, but I'm struggling with all this right now."

And with that, he left.

DARKNESS

Jeff and Clare were left staring at each other after Bobby left.

"Do you think we're wrong about humble, hungry, and smart?" Jeff asked.

Clare took a deep breath. "I don't know. I mean, it seems too obvious to be wrong. If you take away any of those qualities, you've got someone you're not going to want to work with. But maybe it's too idealistic."

Against every instinct he had to keep the conversation going, Jeff decided that time and distance might be best.

"Let's pick this up tomorrow when we're not feeling so overwhelmed."

Clare was more than amenable to the suggestion.

That night Jeff and Maurine put the kids to bed and had a long talk about work. After he had explained the situation to her, she gave him the best advice he had received in years.

"Don't be a moron, honey," she said without a hint of irony. "Just because it's simple doesn't mean it's not right."

"So what do I tell Bobby?" Jeff countered, putting practical matters before theoretical ones. "He's pissed."

Maurine didn't hesitate. "Tell him *he's* being a moron. This guy, Ted Montgomery—"

Jeff corrected her. "Marchbanks."

"Whatever. Ted Marchbanks would be terrible to work with. Even I know from my work in advertising and from volunteering at school or at church that you get more done with three people who fit together than with a fourth who doesn't belong. And more than anything else, a person needs humility to belong."

Now Jeff was playing devil's advocate. "We don't really know for sure that Ted isn't humble."

"Are you serious?" she asked kindly and incredulously. "Everything you said tells me that this guy is a complete politician."

Jeff's eyes went wide at the accuracy of Maurine's assessment.

"And you know what happens when you hire a politician?" she asked rhetorically. "Politics. Complications. Ego. If Uncle Bob is anything, he's not a politician."

Before Jeff could respond, Maurine finished. "And from everything I know about Bobby, the last person he'd want to work with is a politician."

Jeff knew that his wife was right. Unfortunately, she refused to come to work with him the next morning to tell Bobby that he was a moron.

FIRST LIGHT

Jeff went to work early, not sure what he was going to do. When Clare arrived, he sat down and replayed much of the conversation he had with Maurine the night before.

"In theory, it all makes sense," she agreed. "But the practical reality we're dealing with here makes it easy to throw it all out and run the business like every other generic company out there."

Jeff stood up, frowning. "What we need is to stop thinking about Ted Marchbanks and decide whether we're committed to this model. Whether it works in practice."

"I don't know how to do that. And how we can prove it to Bobby?" Clare responded.

Jeff seemed to have a revelation. "What if we used it to figure out the Oak Ridge situation?"

"What do you mean?" she asked.

"I mean, let's look at the people involved and see if humble, hungry, and smart helps us understand what happened there and how to solve it."

"Shouldn't we have Bobby here?"

Jeff winced. "Probably. If you think he can let go of the Ted thing for a half hour."

"I can make him do that."

And with that Jeff called Bobby and asked him to come by as soon as he arrived at the office.

"How about fifteen seconds?" Bobby asked with just a hint of bitterness in his voice. "I'm just down the hall."

Three minutes later, he came in. "Sorry it took so long. I had to pee."

Jeff was glad to see that some of Bobby's humor was beginning to resurface.

Bobby sat down and saw that Clare was standing at the whiteboard drawing a map of the Oak Ridge project teams, beginning with Nancy and Craig and including the foremen and key project managers below them, nine people in all.

"What are we doing here?" Bobby asked, with no hint of humor.

Jeff took a deep breath. "Bobby, we have to decide whether this humble, hungry, and smart thing works in reality or whether it's just a theoretical idea that makes our lives harder."

Bobby sat up a little in his chair. "I like that. Let's do it."

Clare went to the board and circled *Nancy*. "Okay, we've already agreed that Nancy isn't very good when it comes to understanding people, but she's not really arrogant or lazy. She's humble and hungry, but not smart. She makes a lot of messes that have to be cleaned up."

Bobby nodded his agreement.

"So let's look at her team," Clare suggested.

The executives reviewed the three people below Nancy, including the two foremen who left and had to be replaced, Pedro and Carl. As it turned out, Pedro was a clear team player, matching up with all three qualities. Carl, on the other hand, lacked hunger in a significant way.

"This is why Craig's guys were so pissed about falling behind," Bobby announced. "I'll bet if we'd gotten rid of Carl, we could have kept Pedro."

Jeff was glad that the assessments were making sense, but he hadn't won Bobby over quite yet. So he pushed harder. "Let's keep going, Clare."

"Okay, let's talk about Craig and his team," she announced. "How does he stack up?"

Jeff was glad to see that Bobby went first. "Craig's definitely hungry. He might be the hardest working guy I've got. I've never had to tell him to do something, and he's always thinking of how he can do more to help everyone else."

Jeff weighed in now. "And do you think he's humble? He doesn't seem arrogant to me."

Bobby nodded. "Very low maintenance. Doesn't want attention. Isn't a self-promoter at all. Sometimes I ignore him because there are rarely problems in his area."

"Is he smart?" Clare asked.

Jeff looked at Bobby for an answer.

"Well, I'm convinced that the problems at Oak Ridge weren't his fault, if that's what you mean." He paused, looking back at Jeff. "You've been dealing with him lately. What's your take?"

"I certainly don't think Craig is a world-class diplomat, like Ted. He calls things as he sees them, and he doesn't mince his words. But I like that. I'm curious about what his employees think of him."

"They'd do anything for him," Bobby said proudly. "Craig's guys love him. He knows when someone needs their butt kicked a little and when someone needs a pat on the back. The guy's a prince."

Clare added, "Every year he gets one of the highest rankings from employees." She paused for a moment as something occurred to her. "You know, if Craig ever left, I bet a dozen or more people would follow him wherever he went."

Jeff moved the conversation forward. "Okay, Craig is smart, and he's a team player. Let's keep going. What about his people?"

Clare circled the next name on the board. "Okay, what about Brandon?"

Clare knew Brandon, one of Craig's foremen, and was providing her own insights into his level of hunger, when suddenly Bobby interrupted.

"Hold on a second." He seemed almost angry, but not quite.

Jeff and Clare looked at him.

"What are we, idiots?" Bobby asked loudly.

Jeff was suddenly preparing to go toe-to-toe with Bobby, until he explained.

"Why don't we hire Craig?"

"He already works here," Clare explained.

"Come on, Clare. I mean, why don't we make him part of our team?"

Jeff was more than a little surprised. "Craig?"

"Yeah, why not?" Bobby responded.

"I guess I just never thought of him as someone at that level."

Bobby shot back. "Hey, the guy knows the business backward and forward. So, if you're serious about humble, hungry, and smart, he would be a no-brainer."

Jeff couldn't tell if Bobby was serious or challenging Jeff's commitment to the model.

Thankfully, Clare weighed in. "He's just so different than Ted. I mean, one guy ran a sixty-million-dollar division of a company and has years of experience working at high levels, and the other guy. . . ."

She paused, and didn't finish the sentence.

Bobby did. "And the other guy has been here proving himself for ten years and we know that he's all about teamwork."

Jeff looked at Bobby. "Do you think he's got the maturity? Can he handle a higher level of stress and more balls to juggle?"

Bobby thought about it. "I'd say 'no' if you meant that he had to go work for another company without any help. But here, with our help, I have no doubt that he'd be fine."

"Really?" Clare asked.

Bobby didn't hesitate. "Absolutely." And then he said something that closed the deal. "And you know he'd fit in with us, much better than Ted Marchbanks."

Jeff was shocked. "So you agree that Ted wasn't an ideal fit?"

Bobby shrugged in a guilty way. "I had my doubts about his humility. But when you're desperate—"

Clare finished his sentence for him. "You do stupid things."

NANCY

s much as Jeff wanted to bring the discussion to a close and declare a victory, he had a nagging concern.

"So what about Nancy?" he asked, without any context.

"What do you mean?" Clare responded.

"I mean, when we have someone like her who's lacking in one of the three areas, what do we do about that?"

No one had a quick answer, so Jeff continued. "We know we're not just going to fire her. But how do we do our best to give her a chance to be a real team player?"

Clare offered a half-hearted suggestion. "Well, there are coaches I know who do one-on-one counseling."

Bobby shook his head. "No, that doesn't usually work. It takes months and only isolates people. It seems like most of them just use it to prepare for their next job."

"I'd have to agree," said Jeff.

Clare didn't offer up an argument, but weighed in. "What we need is something more direct and actionable. Something that gives us a quick sense of whether she really wants to change or has the capacity for it."

Jeff had an idea. "Hey, why don't we just interview her?"

"What do you mean?" Bobby was confused.

"Why don't I just sit down with Nancy and talk to her the way I talked to Ted?" Jeff didn't wait for a response. "If she doesn't want to be here, she'll probably make that clear. She might even decide to leave on her own."

Bobby looked deflated. "Oh, I really don't want to lose anyone else." Before Clare could pounce on him, he continued. "But if that's what needs to happen, I'm okay with it."

Clare patted her colleague on the head.

Jeff continued. "I won't make it a witch hunt or anything. I'll just describe what we're trying to do with the culture, and see if she has the stomach for it."

"And what if she says she's up for it?" Bobby asked. "How do we teach her to be smarter?"

"That's a high-class problem, my friend," Clare announced. "If Attila the Hun walked into this office right now and convinced me that he really wanted to get better dealing with people, I know we could do it. Most training and development comes down to how much a person wants to change."

Jeff hoped Nancy would be easier than Attila the Hun.

PART FIVE

Indicators

RE-INTERVIEWING

ancy came to Jeff's office a little after lunch. Jeff asked her to clear the rest of her day, "just in case." He knew the request might unnerve her since she didn't know the purpose of the meeting. But he decided it would be worth the temporary stress to have enough time to discern whether she was open to change and perhaps to get the process started.

Nancy sat down in one of the chairs facing Uncle Bob's big desk, and Jeff thought she seemed less than happy to be there.

"How are you, Nancy?" he asked, with considerable interest and kindness.

"I'm fine, Jeff." Her response was just barely more than curt. "How do you like your new job?"

Though she didn't seem to be interested in an answer, Jeff responded as though she were dying to know. "It's a little more challenging than I thought, but I've got better people working with me than I could have imagined."

Nancy nodded, as if to say *good for you.*

Jeff dove in, determined to be as confident as he was kind. "So, the reason I asked you to come see me is to talk to you about your career at VB and your development."

She seemed confused and detached all at once.

Jeff thought about his conversation with Ted and went for broke. "Nancy, you know that teamwork is one of our values and that it's really important to Bob, right along with safety and quality."

She nodded. Nothing else.

Jeff went on. "Well, we're going to continue that focus, and even step it up a little around teamwork, especially given the fact that we're going to be taking on a lot more work this year, with the hotel in St. Helena and the wing at Queen of the Valley Hospital."

He continued. "The only way we're going to be able to staff those projects and get them done is if we make sure that everyone is working as a team."

Jeff noticed that Nancy began to roll her eyes just briefly, which provoked him to address her objections. "Now, this isn't anything touchy-feely. You don't know me, Nancy, but I'm not a fan of hugging or holding hands or catching people falling out of a tree."

For the first time, he saw the glimpse of a smile from Nancy. It was gone as fast as it appeared.

"Anyway, I want to make sure that all of the people we hire, and all the people who work here, understand what we mean by being a team player and that they really want to be one. And I'm starting with people in leadership positions."

More nodding from Nancy, but no sign of interest. Jeff knew that was about to change.

"So, Clare and Bobby and I have been working hard lately to define exactly what we mean by a team player, and we've settled on three words."

Jeff stood and went to the whiteboard. "Team players have three things in common. They are humble, hungry, and smart." He wrote the words on the whiteboard and returned to his chair.

Nothing from Nancy, so Jeff pushed on.

"Humble is pretty obvious. We can't abide big egos. Hungry is all about working hard and being passionate about our work. And smart has to do with being aware of the people around you and dealing with them in a positive, functional way."

It was clear that Nancy was beginning to process things in her mind, but she wasn't ready to make any comments. So Jeff asked the sixty-four-thousand-dollar question.

"How do you think you stack up against these qualities?"

Now Nancy moved in her chair.

To make it easier for her to loosen up, Jeff added, "And we all struggle in one or more of these areas from time to time."

That seemed to be the impetus Nancy needed.

"Well, anyone that works with me for more than a few minutes will say I'm hungry. That would be my strongest area, I'm sure." Nancy paused to check on Jeff's reaction.

He nodded and added, "I'd say that's obvious."

"And though Craig might disagree, I don't think that being humble is a problem for me. I mean, that might sound arrogant, but I don't think I have a particularly big ego."

"Actually," Jeff replied, "Craig said the same thing about you."

Nancy seemed genuinely surprised. "Really?"

"Absolutely. He told me himself."

With a slightly but undeniably higher level of confidence, she began, "Well then, I'd have to say that I'm not that good at social interaction, which is the smart part, right?"

Jeff nodded. "That's right." He decided not to say anything else, wanting Nancy to continue.

She did. "Frankly, I just don't spend a lot of energy on being nice all the time. I'd rather focus on getting things done. Some people don't like that, I guess."

Jeff was slightly incredulous. "Let me get this straight, Nancy. You think it's a waste of energy to be nice to people?"

Nancy didn't answer him, so he continued.

"We're not talking about giving each other back rubs and hugs."

Nancy laughed. "Okay, it's not that I don't want to be nice." She seemed to be searching for a way to explain her way out of the situation. "I don't know."

Jeff asked his next question gently. "Nancy, do you know how others receive the things you say to them?"

After considering the question for a moment, she responded. "The thing is, people who aren't socially smart probably aren't very good at knowing it. Otherwise, they'd be better at it."

Jeff laughed. "I'd say you're right about that."

Nancy went on. "So, as much as I'd like to say that I'm willing to work on that . . . ,"

She paused, and Jeff thought she was going to tell him that she wasn't interested in whatever he was offering.

And then she finished. "I'm going to need help from someone to get better." She paused, and then said the three most important words of all: "But I'll try."

Jeff wanted to jump up and hug Nancy, but figured she'd probably throw him to the floor.

"Nancy, that's all I can ask."

ABOUT A WEEK LATER

Jeff made Craig's hiring official within two days, and the reaction from employees was overwhelmingly positive. That was enough to make the other three members of the executive team glad not to have hired Ted Marchbanks. But it wouldn't be the only thing.

A few days after Ted had pulled himself out as a candidate for the job at VB, one of the "unauthorized references" called. This was a former employee at NBC who knew of Ted well. Her name was Dani, and she was Kim's brother's girlfriend's sister. At first, she seemed less than forthcoming, until Jeff explained, "Actually, Ted decided not to pursue a job here after all."

"All right then," Dani explained, "then I guess you don't need me."

Before she could hang up, Jeff caught her. "Can I ask you one quick question, Dani, just between you and me. You don't have to answer if you don't want to."

After a moment, she relented. "Sure. What's your question?"

"Well, our culture is extremely," he paused, searching for a word or phrase that would be accurate but not showy. He settled on "down-to-earth and unpretentious."

He continued. "We were concerned that Ted might have been a little too," again he paused, "sophisticated for us, if you know what I mean."

Dani laughed. "Oh, I think I know what you mean."

Before Jeff could say anything, she went on. "And let's just say that down-to-earth wouldn't be how I would describe Ted."

"Okay," Jeff said. "I appreciate your honesty."

A few days later, Clare's connection came through. He was one of Ted's former clients, and he was less delicate than Dani. "Listen, Jeff. I know Bob Shanley, and he and Ted are not at all alike when it comes to personality or culture. You dodged a bullet there, if you ask me. We can just leave it at that."

Clare and Bobby were enormously relieved when they heard about those references. Even so, occasionally, one of the three executives was likely to express some doubt about the humble, hungry, smart system and whether it would be enough. On those days, the other leaders would convince them to trust the model.

Of course, the proof would be in the pudding.

ABOUT A MONTH LATER

Less than thirty days after moving Craig into the "executive suite" and everyone committing fully to the new hiring model, everything at VB had changed completely. All open positions had been hired with ideal team players, and the projects were both way ahead of schedule. And every single employee who lacked humility, hunger, and smarts had chosen to leave the company on their own, with no animosity.

Jeff was so happy that he was literally flying around the offices, his feet completely off the ground. And that's how he knew that he was dreaming.

When he woke up, Jeff was immediately thinking about the hospital project and whether it would ever be adequately staffed. Aside from that and a handful of other tactical issues, Jeff was generally pleased with the process that was underway at the company. Perhaps the most important part of that process was the new hiring program that Clare had put in place.

Based on what she and her colleagues had learned in the process of coming up with humble, hungry, and smart, and the experience of testing it with Ted and others, Clare had launched a remarkably simple training program for everyone involved in the hiring process. From recruiting team players to vetting them during interviews, all hiring managers understood the basics of humble, hungry, and smart and their roles in making the model a reality at VB.

As for the hiring itself, they were still not where they wanted to be in terms of numbers. However, that concern was offset by the quality of a few of the more senior people they had hired—people who would have key roles at the hotel and the hospital. With them on board, Clare felt that hiring would get easier because she would have more people out there looking for the kind of employees who fit the company's culture.

One of the biggest moral victories the team had achieved was rehiring Pedro, one of the foremen who had quit amidst the stress and politics at Oak Ridge. The key to bringing him back was Bobby's passion around the new culture being built at VB, and Nancy's humility.

At Jeff's urging, Nancy sat down with Pedro and explained to him how she had let him down in not confronting the issues that had festered at Oak Ridge. Pedro would later tell Bobby that she had never spoken to him that way before, and that if she were any indication of what was happening at the company, he would be glad to be a part of it.

Jeff had been so pleased with Nancy's progress that he decided to take three full days and meet with every one of the company's seventeen foremen and project leads for a re-interview. For those that seemed to have no shortfalls in humble, hungry, or smart, Jeff used the discussion to reinforce his commitment to hiring and nurturing team players and to ensure that every VB leader was ready to make it his or her responsibility to protect the culture.

For the handful of leaders who had clear shortfalls in humble, hungry, or smart, Jeff took a more direct approach. After getting agreement on their need for improvement in one or more of the areas, he kindly assured them of three things. First, improvement was not an option. Second, they would have plenty of support in their development. Third, if they decided to opt out, that would be okay.

Only two people wanted to leave. One of them Jeff convinced to stay, knowing that her motivation for leaving was just the shame of being called on her issue. The other one, a particularly difficult foreman named Tom, got no argument from Jeff at all. Clare was beside herself with relief when Jeff explained that Tom would be leaving, on his own.

"You know," she said to Jeff after the last of his re-interviews, "this isn't going to be easy, these two projects."

Jeff smiled and didn't disagree with her.

"But I'm as excited as I've been in years."

"Me too," Jeff agreed. "Me too."

ABOUT SIX MONTHS LATER

Even though the new cultural model was now firmly in place, Jeff was concerned that the hospital and hotel projects weren't going very smoothly.

Bobby was not so concerned. "That's okay, boss. No projects go smoothly. This is par for the course."

Still, Jeff had hoped everything would be markedly better than normal. "I just feel like things should be much more predictable by now."

As for the leaders who had been re-interviewed by Jeff and agreed to a development plan, only one had to be let go when it became clear that hunger just wasn't part of his makeup. The others were making progress, though Clare wasn't sure that one or two of them would be there for the long term.

This also troubled Jeff, who thought that personnel situations would be completely resolved by now.

"Come on, Jeff," Clare exhorted him. "We're almost where we need to be on hiring, the clients aren't even close to firing us, and everything is trending in the right direction. If you had told me six months ago that we'd still be in business at this point, I might have bet against you."

Though he couldn't argue with her assertion, it still bothered Jeff that a couple of people who might not be team players still worked at VB.

"Yes," Clare explained, "and we know exactly who they are, and what needs to be done to fix it. You have to remember how we were a year ago, and how most companies work."

As he had grown accustomed to doing since his promotion, Craig gently scolded Jeff. "Stop making the perfect enemy of the good."

Bobby piled on. "Yeah. You're not a consultant anymore. This is reality, and I'll take it."

Though Jeff took great consolation in the reassurance of his experienced peers, he knew that he'd always be a little paranoid. And being a little paranoid was part of his job, he decided. Still, he wasn't about to change course. He had placed his bet, and needed to let it play out over time.

ABOUT A YEAR LATER

On the one-year anniversary of Bob's surgery, many aspects of VB had changed substantially, and others had stayed largely the same.

Bob himself was healthy and was enjoying real retirement, though he occasionally stopped by the office with his wife, Karen, for a visit. Each time, he avoided talking too much business with Jeff, limiting his work-related comments to teasing him, often saying, "See, I told you it would be okay."

Craig was firmly entrenched as an executive, working closely with Bobby on the day-to-day oversight of the two major projects and even managing Nancy Morris directly, often calling her his best employee. The group of four executives had become closer with the addition of Craig, and couldn't imagine not having him on the team.

But the biggest change that the humble, hungry, and smart model had made could be seen most starkly in human resources—not the department, but the function. Though Clare and her small staff were certainly involved in maintaining the culture, Jeff had made it clear that his leadership team, and their direct reports, were responsible for ensuring that VB stayed humble, hungry, and smart. He also constantly reminded them that there was nothing theoretical or touchy-feely about it.

From interviews and orientation to performance reviews and compensation decisions, "the three virtues," as they came to be known, were to be regular topics of conversation. And, of course, there was plenty of hands-on, practical training around the five behavioral manifestations of teamwork: trust, conflict, commitment, accountability, and results. Those courses had become much more effective with participants who shared the three underlying virtues.

From a practical standpoint, there were a few indicators that VB's business had changed as a result of the clarity around teamwork. First, recruiting had shifted largely away from headhunters and outside agencies as more and more employees, from contractors to foremen, sought out jobs at VB through friends and references.

Second, morale at the company was undeniably higher, and turnover had dropped markedly. But Jeff was adamant that it shouldn't go away completely: "If no one is leaving or being asked to leave, then we're probably not truly living these values."

Finally, and most importantly from the standpoint of proof that the model worked, client satisfaction at the hospital and the hotel were better than Jeff and his team could have expected. Though fires had to be fought and unexpected challenges surfaced at inopportune times, the way the company rallied and addressed those issues no longer inspired panic and heroism. A new confidence, even in the messiest situations, permeated the offices and worksites of Valley Builders.

Of all the leaders at VB, it was Bobby who most accurately and indelicately explained the benefits of how humble, hungry, and smart had changed the company.

At the end of the executive team's fourth-quarter off-site meeting, as the four leaders were assessing the overall health of the organization, Bobby announced, "If you ask me, the best thing that's happened in the last year is that we've almost become a jackass-free zone. No matter what happens, and what challenge we might face, give me a roomful of people who aren't jackasses, and I'll be happy to take it on."

And with that, he threw a T-shirt at Jeff, who held it up to reveal the word *jackass* with a circle around it and a line through it.

Though Jeff knew he would never actually wear that shirt, he kept it in his drawer at work as a reminder of his primary responsibility as the company's leader.

The Model

THE THREE VIRTUES OF
AN IDEAL TEAM PLAYER

his section of the book is about understanding the ideal team player model, what it means, where it comes from, and how it can be put to practical use. Let's start with the big picture.

In his classic book, *Good To Great*, Jim Collins talks about the importance of successful companies getting "the right people on the bus," a euphemism for hiring and retaining employees who fit a company's culture. It is a concept that is relatively simple and makes perfect sense, yet somehow it is often overlooked, as too many leaders hire mostly for competency and technical skills.

For organizations seriously committed to making teamwork a cultural reality, I'm convinced that "the right people" are the ones who have the three virtues in common—humility, hunger, and people smarts. I refer to these as virtues because the word *virtue* is a synonym for the nouns *quality* and *asset*, but it also connotes the idea of integrity and morality. Humility, which is the most important of the three, is certainly a virtue in the deepest sense of the word. Hunger and people smarts fall more into the quality or asset category. So, the word *virtue* best captures them all.

Of course, to recognize and cultivate humble, hungry, and smart team members, or to become one yourself, you first need to understand exactly what these deceptively simple words mean and how *all three together* make up the essential virtues of an ideal team player.

DEFINING THE THREE VIRTUES

HUMBLE

In the context of teamwork, humility is largely what it seems to be. Great team players lack excessive ego or concerns about status. They are quick to point out the contributions of others and slow to seek attention for their own. They share credit, emphasize team over self, and define success collectively rather than individually. It is no great surprise, then, that humility is the single greatest and most indispensable attribute of being a team player.

What's amazing is that so many leaders who value teamwork will tolerate people who aren't

> Humility is the single greatest and most indispensable attribute of being a team player.

humble. They reluctantly hire self-centered people and then justify it simply because those people have desired skills. Or, they see arrogant behavior in an employee and fail to confront it, often citing that person's individual contributions as an excuse. The problem, of course, is that leaders aren't considering the effect that an arrogant, self-centered person has on the overall performance of the team. This happens in sports, business, and every other kind of team venture.

There are two basic types of people who lack humility, and it's important, even critical, to understand them, because they look quite different from one another and impact a team differently. The most obvious kind is the overtly arrogant people who make everything about them. They are easy to identify because they tend to boast and soak up attention. This is the classically ego-driven type and it diminishes teamwork by fostering resentment, division, and politics. Most of us have seen plenty of this behavior in our careers.

The next type is much less dangerous, but still worth understanding. These are the people who lack self-confidence but are generous and positive with others. They tend to discount their own talents and contributions, and so others mistakenly see them as humble. But this is not humility. While they are certainly not arrogant, their lack of understanding of their own worth is also a violation of humility. Truly humble people do not see themselves as greater than they are, but neither do they discount their talents and contributions. C.S. Lewis addressed this misunderstanding about humility when he said "Humility isn't thinking less of yourself, but thinking of yourself less."

A person who has a disproportionately deflated sense of self-worth often hurts teams by not advocating for their own ideas or by failing to call attention to problems that they see. Though this kind of lack of humility is less obtrusive and obvious than the other, more negative types, it detracts from optimal team performance nonetheless.

What both of these types have in common is insecurity. Insecurity makes some people project overconfidence, and others discount their own talents. And while these types are not equal when it comes to creating problems on a team, they each diminish performance.

HUNGRY

Hungry people are always looking for more. More things to do. More to learn. More responsibility to take on. Hungry people almost never have to be pushed by a manager to work harder because they are self-motivated and diligent. They are constantly thinking about the next step and the next opportunity. And they loathe the idea that they might be perceived as slackers.

It's not difficult to understand why hungry people are great to have on a team, but it's important to realize that some types of hunger are not good for a team and are even unhealthy. In some people, hunger can be directed in a selfish way that is not for the good of the team but for the individual. And in some people, hunger can be taken to an extreme where work becomes too important, consuming the identity of an employee and dominating their life. When I refer to hunger here, I'm thinking about the healthy kind—a manageable and sustainable commitment to doing a job well and going above and beyond when it is truly required.

> Hungry people almost never have to be pushed by a manager to work harder because they are self-motivated and diligent.

Okay, few team leaders will knowingly ignore a lack of hunger in their people, most likely because unproductive, dispassionate people tend to stand out and create obvious problems on a team. Unfortunately, undiscerning leaders too often hire these people because most candidates know how to falsely project a sense of hunger during standard interviews. As a result, those leaders find themselves spending inordinate amounts of time trying to motivate, punish, or dismiss non-hungry team members once they're on board.

SMART

Of the three virtues, this one needs the most clarification because it is not what it might seem; it is not about intellectual capacity. In the context of a team, *smart* simply refers to a person's common sense about people. It has everything to do with the ability to be interpersonally appropriate and aware. Smart people tend to know what is happening in a group situation and how to deal with others in the most effective way. They ask good questions, listen to what others are saying, and stay engaged in conversations intently.

Some might refer to this as emotional intelligence, which wouldn't be a bad comparison, but smart is probably a little simpler than that. Smart people just have good judgment and intuition around the subtleties of group dynamics and the impact of their words and actions. As a result, they don't say and do things—or fail to say and do things— without knowing the likely responses of their colleagues.

> Smart simply refers to a person's common sense about people.

Keep in mind that being smart doesn't necessarily imply good intentions. Smart people can use their talents for good or ill purposes. In fact, some of the most dangerous people in history have been noted for being interpersonally smart.

THE THREE VIRTUES COMBINED

If you're thinking that these three virtues seem somewhat obvious, I would be the first to agree with you. Looking at them one by one, I'm reluctant to present them in any way that would suggest that I believe they are novel or new. What makes humble, hungry, and smart powerful and unique is not the individual attributes themselves, but rather the required combination of all three. If even one is missing in a team member, teamwork becomes significantly more difficult, and sometimes not possible. Before we get into that, this would probably be a good time to explain how the ideal team player model came to be.

> What makes humble, hungry, and smart powerful and unique is not the individual attributes themselves, but rather the required combination of all three.

THE HISTORY OF
THE MODEL

ack in 1997, a group of colleagues and I started our management consulting firm, The Table Group. Because we had worked together in a department I led in a previous company, we had an easy time agreeing on our core values: humble, hungry, and smart. These were the principles that guided our department previously, and we wanted to maintain them in our new firm. So we committed to hiring only people who embodied these concepts and to avoid making any operational or strategic decisions that violated them.

In the consulting work we did with clients, we not only helped leaders build better teams, but we also assisted them in clarifying everything from their strategies, tactics, roles, responsibilities, meetings, and, most important for this conversation, values. In the course of discussing values, clients would inevitably ask us about ours at The Table Group.

Now, we didn't publicize humble, hungry, and smart. They were nowhere to be found on our website or in any of our collateral. We felt that as long as we understood and stayed true to them, no one else really needed to understand them. However, when clients asked us, we felt compelled to share them. And when we explained humble, hungry, and smart, something strange would often happen: clients would declare that they were going to adopt those values, too.

Of course, we would immediately protest and explain that an organization's values can't be copied or borrowed; they need to be true reflections of the unique history and culture of that organization. We often attributed our clients' interest in our values to expediency, or perhaps even laziness—their desire to grab the first set of positive-sounding words, so that they could declare their search for values over. Well, we eventually discovered we were wrong about their motivation and that there was a logical explanation why our clients wanted to adopt humble, hungry, and smart.

First, our firm's culture was all about teamwork, both in what we did with clients and in how we tried to behave internally, because we had always vowed to practice what we preached. Second, virtually all the companies that engaged our firm were already interested in teamwork, which makes sense given that we were best known for the book *The Five Dysfunctions of a Team*. So, it shouldn't have been terribly surprising to think that our hiring criteria and core values would make up the very definition of a team player, even if we didn't realize it at the time.

Once we made this realization, we started to look at the relevance of humble, hungry, and smart for other organizations in a different way. Those words weren't necessarily core values, but they were critical hiring and development criteria for any organization that wanted teamwork to be central to its operations.

To make sure we weren't deluding ourselves, we asked the question, *Could a person fully practice the five behaviors at the heart of teamwork (see the model on page 214) if he or she didn't buy into the idea of being humble, hungry, and smart?*

The answer was a resounding *no*.

A person who is not humble will not be able to be vulnerable and build trust, making them unable to engage in honest conflict and hold others accountable. And they'll have a hard time committing to decisions that don't serve their interests. A colleague who lacks hunger will not be willing to engage in uncomfortable conflict, hold peers accountable for their behaviors, or do whatever it takes to achieve results, choosing instead to take an easier path. And a person who is not smart about people will most likely create unnecessary problems in the entire teambuilding process, especially when it comes to tactfully engaging in productive conflict and holding people accountable for behaviors.

After reviewing, discussing, and using the model in our own firm and seeing our clients try to adopt it in theirs, we became convinced that any leader who wants to make teamwork a reality should find and/or develop people who are humble, hungry, and smart. To do all of this, leaders need to understand how these qualities work together and what happens when one or more of them are missing.

THE IDEAL TEAM
PLAYER MODEL

The model on the following page depicts the intersections between humble, hungry, and smart, with the central overlapping piece representing the combined qualities of an ideal team player. That is not to imply that a person in that middle section will be consistently perfect in all of these virtues, or in any one of them, for that matter. No one is perfect. Even a person who is humble, hungry, and smart occasionally has a bad day, or a bad week, or even a bad time in their life. These are not permanent characteristics embedded in a person's DNA; rather, they are developed and maintained through life experiences and personal choices at home and at work.

When team members are adequately strong in each of these areas—when they possess significant humility, hunger, and people smarts—they enable teamwork by making it relatively easy for members to overcome the five dysfunctions of a team (see model on page 214). That means they'll be more likely to be vulnerable and build trust, engage in productive but uncomfortable conflict with team members, commit to group decisions even if they initially disagree, hold their peers accountable when they see performance gaps that can be addressed, and put the results of the team ahead of their own needs.

Only humble, hungry, and smart people can do those things without a great deal of coaching. Those who don't have all three virtues are going to require significantly more time, attention, and patience from their managers.

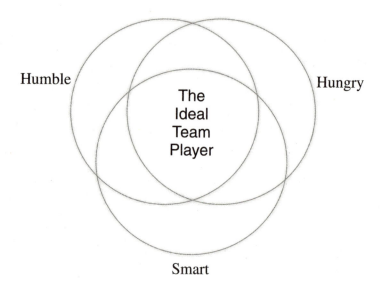

Let's take a look at the various categories of people, starting with those who have none of the required qualities and moving to the ideal team players who have all three.

THE CATEGORIES

0 for 3

Those who lack all three qualities, who are markedly deficient in humility, hunger, and people smarts, have little chance of being valuable team members. It would take great effort over a long period of time for them to develop the capacity for all three, let alone two or even one. Fortunately for managers, these people are very easy to identify and rarely slip through interviews and make it onto teams. Unfortunately, life can be very hard for them.

I for 3

For those who lack two of the three in a big way, it's also going to be an uphill battle—not impossible, but not easy. Let's look at these three categories, the ones involving a team member who is only humble, hungry, or smart.

Humble Only: The Pawn

People who are only humble but not at all hungry or smart are the "pawns" on a team. They are pleasant, kind-hearted, unassuming people who just don't feel a great need to get things done and don't have the ability to build effective relationships with colleagues. They often get left out of conversations and activities, and have little impact on the performance of a team. Pawns don't make waves, so they can survive for quite a long time on teams that value harmony and don't demand performance.

Hungry Only: The Bulldozer

People who are hungry but not at all humble or smart can be thought of as "bulldozers." These people will be determined to get things done, but with a focus on their own interests and with no understanding or concern for how their actions impact others. Bulldozers are quick destroyers of teams.

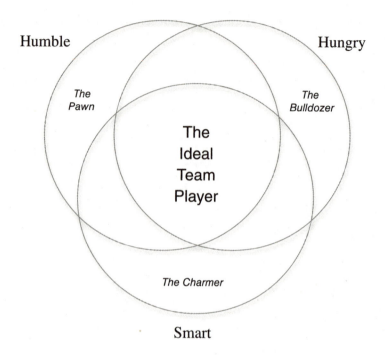

Fortunately, unlike pawns, they stand out and can be easily identified and removed by leaders who truly value teamwork. However, in organizations that place a premium on production alone, bulldozers can thrive and go uncorrected for long periods of time.

Smart Only: The Charmer

People who are smart but sorely lacking in humility and hunger are "charmers." They can be entertaining and even likeable for a while, but have little interest in the long-term well-being of the team or their colleagues. Their social skills can sometimes help them survive longer than bulldozers or pawns, but because their contributions to the team are negligible, they often wear out their welcome quickly.

2 for 3

The next three categories that we'll explore represent people who are more difficult to identify because the strengths associated with them often camouflage their weaknesses. Team members who fit into these categories lack only one of the three traits and thus have a little higher likelihood of overcoming their challenges and becoming ideal team players. Still, lacking even one in a serious way can impede the team-building process.

Humble and Hungry, but Not Smart: The Accidental Mess-Maker

People who are humble and hungry but decidedly not smart are the "accidental mess-makers." They genuinely want to serve the team and are not interested in getting a disproportionate amount of attention and credit. However, their lack of understanding of how their words and actions are received by others will lead them to inadvertently create interpersonal problems on the team. While colleagues will respect their work ethic and sincere desire to be helpful, those colleagues can get tired of having to clean up the emotional and interpersonal problems that accidental mess-makers so often leave behind. In the fable, Nancy was the accidental mess-maker—a relatively egoless, hard-working employee who lacked interpersonal dexterity and created unnecessary problems on the team.

169

Though the accidental mess-maker can definitely be a problem, of the three types that lack just one of the characteristics of an ideal team player, this is the least dangerous to a team, as accidental mess-makers have no bad intentions and can usually take corrective feedback in good humor.

Humble and Smart, but Not Hungry: The Lovable Slacker
People who are humble and smart but not adequately hungry are the "lovable slackers." They aren't looking for undeserved attention, and they are adept at working with and caring about colleagues. Unfortunately, they tend to do only as much as they are asked, and rarely seek to take on more work or volunteer for extra assignments. Moreover, they have limited passion for the work the team is doing. Because they are generally charming and positive, it's easy for leaders to shy away from confronting or removing lovable slackers. After all, they're lovable.

In the fable, a minor character referred to as Tommy was a lovable slacker. He was neither a jerk nor a complete sloth, but did only what was expected of him and no more. Tommy had passion about various pursuits in his life, but none of this passion was directed at work.

Lovable slackers need significant motivation and oversight, making them a drag on the team's performance, more so than the accidental mess-makers. But they don't represent the most dangerous of the three types who lack one of the virtues; that would be the skillful politician.

Hungry and Smart, but Not Humble: The Skillful Politician
People who are hungry and smart but lack humility are the "skillful politicians." These people are cleverly ambitious

170

and willing to work extremely hard, but only in as much as it will benefit them personally. Unfortunately, because they are so smart, skillful politicians are very adept at portraying themselves as being humble, making it hard for leaders to identify them and address their destructive behaviors. By the time the leader sees what's going on, the politician may have already created a trail of destruction among their more humble colleagues who have been manipulated, discouraged, and scarred. Most of us have worked with plenty of skillful politicians, as they tend to rise in the ranks of companies where leaders reward individual performance over teamwork.

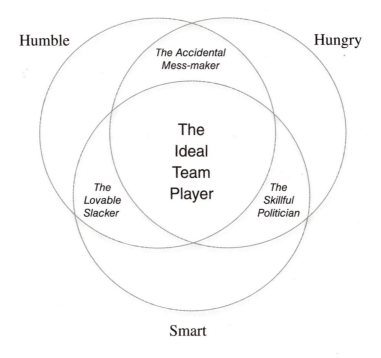

In the fable, Ted Marchbanks was the skillful politician. He was professional, charismatic, and motivated, which is why Jeff and his team almost hired him. Ultimately, Ted turned out to be much more interested in himself than on the people around him.

WARNING: Now is probably a good time for a few important warnings. First, keep in mind that accurately identifying people as bulldozers, charmers, pawns, accidental mess-makers, lovable slackers, or skillful politicians is not always easy, and shouldn't be done flippantly. Wrongly labeling a team member, even in private or jest, can be damaging. Second, don't assign these labels to colleagues who are truly ideal team players simply because they are *relatively* stronger in one of the three areas. For instance, don't refer to an ideal team player who is slightly less hungry than she is humble and smart as a lovable slacker. These classifications are reserved only for people who are *significantly* lacking in one or more of the three traits.

Managers will need to be "smart" about how to use the terms with their employees. And remember, the real purpose of identifying these types is not to pigeonhole people, but to better understand what constitutes ideal team players so we can recognize or develop them on our teams.

3 for 3

Humble, Hungry, Smart: The Ideal Team Player
Ideal team players possess adequate measures of humility, hunger, and people smarts. They have little ego when it comes to needing attention or credit for their contributions,

and they are comfortable sharing their accolades or even occasionally missing out on them. Ideal team players work with a sense of energy, passion, and personal responsibility, taking on whatever they possibly can for the good of the team. Finally, they say and do the right things to help teammates feel appreciated, understood, and included, even when difficult situations arise that require tough love. Most of us can recall having managed or worked with ideal team players in our careers, as they are quite appealing and memorable.

Now that we understand each of the three virtues and how they fit together, we can look at how the model can be applied.

APPLICATION

There are four primary applications of the ideal team player model within an organization: (1) hiring, (2) assessing current employees, (3) developing employees who are lacking in one or more of the virtues, and (4) embedding the model into an organization's culture. Let's look at these one at a time.

APPLICATION #1: HIRING

The most reliable way to ensure that teamwork takes hold in an organization would be to hire only ideal team players. Of course, that is neither possible nor practical, especially considering that most leaders don't have the luxury of creating their teams from scratch. But all leaders can certainly do their best to try to recruit, select, and hire people who are humble, hungry, and smart when an opportunity arises to bring on someone new.

Though it would be nice to have a perfectly reliable, diagnostic tool for accurately identifying and selecting people who are humble, hungry, and smart, no such tool currently exists. However, by doing thorough interviewing and selective reference checking, a manager can hire people with a high degree of confidence that they'll be ideal team players.

The Interview Process

The most important part of interviewing for team players is simply knowing which answers and behaviors are the best indicators of humility, hunger, and people smarts and then making the interview as revealing as possible. There are plenty of books in the world about behavioral interviewing that offer a variety of models and tools. For me, the key is sticking to a few concepts, all of which may seem obvious but are too often overlooked.

Don't Be Generic

This first one is the most obvious of all, as it is largely the point of this section, if not the entire book. Still, it's worth stating. Too many interviews are so generic that they provide little or no insight into specific attributes. Instead, they leave interviewers with extremely general assessments of candidates. "She seems like a nice person. I like her." That would be fine if you were looking for someone to mow your lawn once a week. If you're looking for a team player who is humble, hungry, and smart, being specific about targeted behaviors and attributes is critical. I'll provide examples of the kinds of questions that reveal those behaviors and attributes later in this section.

Debrief Each Interview as a Team

One of the biggest problems I see is a silo approach to interviewing. This happens when a handful of people conduct their own interviews and don't talk about what they've learned until after the entire round of interviews is complete. The problem is that one interview is no more specific or effective than the previous one.

Instead, interviewers should debrief quickly after each interview, specifically around observations related to humility, hunger, and people smarts. For instance, if the first two interviewers agree that the candidate is hungry and smart, the third can focus on humility, taking more time and probing more directly for the unknown piece.

Consider Group Interviews

I often like to talk with candidates in a room with multiple team members. This allows us to debrief more effectively (e.g., "What did you think he meant when he said . . . ?"). This also gives you a sense of how the candidate deals with multiple people at once, which is a critical skill on a team. Some people are much different one-on-one than they are in a group, and you need to know that.

Make Interviews Nontraditional

It is amazing that as we move further into the twenty-first century, most interviews are still the same stilted, rehearsed, and predictable conversations they were forty years ago. The problem is not that they are boring or old fashioned, but rather that they aren't effective for discerning whether a person has the behavioral skills and values that match an organization or a team.

Someone once told me that the best way to know if you should hire a person is to go on a cross-country business trip with him. See how he handles himself in stressful, interactive situations and over long periods of time. While that isn't necessarily practical, I do believe that interviews should incorporate interaction with diverse groups of people in everyday situations and that they should be longer than forty-five minutes.

I like to get out of the office with a candidate and see him deal with people in an unstructured environment. Running an errand at the grocery store or the mall is not a bad idea. Spending time in a car and seeing how he behaves when he's not answering a question helps me understand him better. And remember, whatever I'm doing with that candidate, I'm looking specifically for signs that he is humble, hungry, and smart.

Ask Questions More than Once

I call this the *Law & Order* principle. On that crime show, tough investigators would always seem to ask suspects the same question again and again until the perp admitted to the crime.

Cop: "Did you murder the guy!?"

Perp: "No."

Cop: "Did you murder the guy!?"

Perp: "No."

Cop: "Did you murder the guy!?"

Perp: "Okay, I did it! I did it!"

Yeah, that's an exaggeration, but the same idea can apply to an interview. Asking an interviewee a question once often yields a generically acceptable answer. Asking that question again in a different way might get you a different answer. If you're not sold on the response, ask a third time in a more specific way, and you will often get a more honest answer.

177

Ask What Others Would Say

This one relates somewhat to the previous suggestion. Instead of asking candidates to self-assess a given behavior or characteristic related to humility, hunger, or people smarts, ask them what *others* would say about them. For example, instead of asking someone if he considers himself to be a hard worker, ask him "How would your colleagues describe your work ethic?" Or instead of asking a candidate if she gets along with her colleagues, ask her "How would your manager describe your relationships with your colleagues?" Or here's an interesting one. Instead of asking someone if he is humble, ask, "If I were to ask your colleagues to assess your level of humility, what would they say?"

Some interviewers will think this sounds obvious, but then they'll admit that they don't do it enough. Others will wonder if such a seemingly small change in tactics can make a difference. But there is just something about having to answer on behalf of another person that makes a candidate more honest. Perhaps this has to do with the possibility of the interviewer doing a reference check. Maybe it's a matter of not wanting to misrepresent someone else's views. Whatever the case, it seems to produce more reliable answers.

Ask Candidates to Do Some Real Work

This one won't always be possible, since it depends on the nature of the work. A doctor can't be asked to do surgery before being hired, but a copy editor, an advertising manager, or a management consultant can be given a simulated work project. The point is not to get free work, but rather to see how people perform in real-world situations so you can discern whether they are humble, hungry, and smart.

Don't Ignore Hunches

If you have a doubt about a person's humility, hunger, or smarts, don't ignore it. Keep probing. More often than not, there is something causing that doubt. That's not to discourage keeping an open mind, but erring on the side of assuming that a person has the virtues of a team player is a bad idea. So many times hiring managers look back at the red flags they saw during interviews, the ones they chose to ignore, and regret not taking more time or energy to understand them. While it's never possible to have *complete* confidence in a hire, nagging doubts about a candidate's humility, hunger, or smarts need to be properly explored and discarded before an offer can be made.

Scare People with Sincerity

One of my favorite ways to ensure that I'm hiring people who are humble, hungry, and smart is to come right out and tell them that these are requirements for the job. It is probably wise to wait until the end of the interviewing process to do this, but it may be the most important part. Here's how it works.

You've finished interviewing, debriefing, and doing follow-up interviews, and you're pretty confident that the interviewee is humble, hungry, and smart. But you're not sure. Before making an offer to the candidate, assure him that you are absolutely, fanatically committed to these principles and that if an employee somehow made it through the interview process but did not share that commitment, it would be

179

miserable working there. Let candidates know that they would be called out for their behavior, again and again, and that they'd eventually dread coming to work. Also, assure them that if they *do* fit the humble, hungry, smart description, work will be fantastic for them.

Many people will try to get a job even if they don't fit the company's stated values, but very few will do so if they know that they're going to be held accountable, day in and day out, for behavior that violates the values. Of course, it's important that you follow through on that commitment to the values in the rare occasion that a candidate calls the bluff.

> Many people will try to get a job even if they don't fit the company's stated values, but very few will do so if they know that they're going to be held accountable, day in and day out, for behavior that violates the values.

Interview Questions

Here are a few questions that can help you get at the essence of humble, hungry, and smart.

Humble

"Tell me about the most important accomplishments of your career." Look for more mentions of *we* than *I*. Of course, it isn't about being so simplistic as to count the responses. In the event that someone refers to herself individually more than as a member of a team, probe for whether she was working alone or with others.

"What was the most embarrassing moment in your career? Or the biggest failure?" Look for whether the candidate celebrates that embarrassment or is mortified by it. Humble

people generally aren't afraid to tell their unflattering stories because they're comfortable with being imperfect. Also, look for specifics and real references to the candidate's own culpability.

"How did you handle that embarrassment or failure?" Again, look for specifics about how he accepted responsibility, what he learned from it, and if he actually acted on what he learned.

"What is your greatest weakness?" Yes, this is a tired question, but it's still a great one. The key is to look for answers that are real and a little painful. Candidates who present their weaknesses as strengths ("I take on too much" or "I have a hard time saying no") are often afraid to acknowledge real shortcomings. To avoid this, I think it's a good idea to coach candidates. "I really want to know what you'd like to change about yourself, or better yet, what your best friends would say you need to work on." The key to the answer is not what their weaknesses are (unless of course they're an axe murderer), but if they're comfortable acknowledging something real.

"How do you handle apologies, either giving or accepting them?" Look for and ask for specifics. Humble people are not afraid to say they are sorry, and they accept other people's genuine apologies with grace. People who do this usually have specific stories.

"Tell me about someone who is better than you in an area that really matters to you." Look for the candidate to demonstrate a genuine appreciation for others who have more skill or talent. Humble people are comfortable with this. Ego-driven people often are not.

Hungry

"What is the hardest you've ever worked on something in your life?" Look for specific examples of real but joyful sacrifice. In other words, the candidate isn't complaining, but is grateful for the experience.

"What do you like to do when you're not working?" Look out for too many time-consuming hobbies that suggest the candidate sees the job as a means to do other things. That's not to say that there is one specific kind of activity that is an indicator of not being hungry. And it's certainly not to say that you're looking for someone who has no interests in life outside of work. But a long list of hobbies like extreme skiing, sled dog racing, storm chasing, and shark hunting might just be a red flag when it comes to someone who is not going to put the needs of the team ahead of personal pursuits.

"Did you work hard when you were a teenager?" Look for specifics, usually relating to schoolwork, sports, or jobs. And when it comes to sports, it's not about participation and having fun. Look for examples of difficulty, sacrifice, and hardship. I like to ask people about how hard they worked in high school. Did they really try to do well? Did they have a job? Did they train extraordinarily hard in a sport? You're not looking for one particular answer, but rather for something real that indicates the person has a work ethic. And a work ethic usually, but not always, gets established early in life.

"What kinds of hours do you generally work?" Hardworking people usually don't want to work nine to five, unless their unique life situations demand it. And if they do, they are usually getting additional work done at home. That's not to say that some people aren't stuck in dead-end, nine-to-five

jobs and are itching to get out and do something challenging. But if a candidate is satisfied with a predictable schedule and talks too much about "balance," there's a chance he isn't terribly hungry. Again, not a litmus test, but a red flag. None of this is to advocate that people should prioritize their work over their families. Not at all. It's just that when a candidate focuses a lot on the hours that he's expected to work, he may not be the kind of hungry team player you need.

Smart

Knowing whether a person has people smarts is difficult to discern by asking a specific question. What is more important is observing her general behavior during an interview process and the way she answers questions. That's why it's important to put her in situations that are not like traditional interviews. Observe how she deals with waiters and waitresses, store clerks, and cab drivers. Some people can mask their social awkwardness during a rehearsed interview, but for a longer period of time in a fluid situation, it is much harder.

Having said all that, here are a few questions that might elicit information about whether a person is smart.

"How would you describe your personality?" Look for how accurately the person describes what you are observing and how introspective he is. Smart people generally know themselves and find it interesting to talk about their behavioral strengths and weaknesses. People who seem stumped or surprised by this question might not be terribly smart when it comes to people.

"What do you do that others in your personal life might find annoying?" Everyone annoys someone, sometimes.

183

Especially at home. Smart people are not immune to this. But neither are they in the dark about it. And they tend to moderate these behaviors at work.

"What kind of people annoy you the most, and how do you deal with them?" What you're looking for here are self-awareness and self-control. Smart people know their pet peeves, and they own the fact that some of those pet peeves are their own issues. They also know how to deal with annoying people in a productive, constructive way.

"Would your former colleagues describe you as an empathic person?" or *"Can you give me an example of how you've demonstrated empathy to a teammate?"* Some people use the word *empathetic*. The issue is whether the candidate seems to understand what others are feeling. Now, there are certain personality types that are less empathic than others, and that's fine. What you're looking for here is an indication that the person values empathy and whether he or she has an understanding of his or her own strengths or weaknesses in this area.

Perhaps the most important question that interviewers can ask to ascertain whether a candidate is smart is one that they should ask themselves: Would I want to work with this person every day? Smart candidates generally seem like the kind of people you'd enjoy spending time with on a regular basis. On its own, it's not a reason to hire them, because it doesn't get at humility or hunger. But it's certainly an important hurdle to overcome in the longer process of choosing people to hire.

Candidate References

Beyond the actual interview, there are other ways to get information as to whether a person will be an ideal team player. One of those, as tired and limited as it may seem, is doing reference checks on candidates.

Now, there are many, many people in the world who know a lot more about this than I do. And there are plenty of reasons why reference checks are not easy in this litigious and protective society. But when looked at not as a legal protection but as an informal tool for helping ensure that you don't make your team or the candidate miserable, it can be very helpful. And many of the same principles apply to reference checks that apply to interviews.

Put the Reference Provider at Ease

It's critical that a reference not feel that he is holding the future of the candidate in his hands, because this makes him want to be overly positive or, in many cases, cautious and general. Explain that the purpose of your call is not simply to ask if the candidate was a good employee, but rather whether she would thrive in the job she's interviewing for. In other words, ask the reference to serve as a consultant, one whose job it is to ensure that there is a fit that will benefit everyone. If that sounds dishonest or tricky, consider that it's nothing but the truth. All you want to do is describe the culture of the team the candidate will be joining and find out whether the reference thinks it's a match. Assure the reference that he or she isn't the only

> Ask the reference to serve as a consultant, one whose job it is to ensure that there is a fit that will benefit everyone.

185

person providing input and that everything will be kept confidential and discreet.

Look for Specifics

It's fine to start by asking the reference to give you three or four adjectives that best describe the candidate. Those might be good indicators of humble, hungry, or smart. But spend your time asking about specific behaviors and about how the candidate compared to other people the reference has managed or worked with. Adjust the interview questions from the previous section, and see how they match up with what the candidate said.

Focus on Areas of Doubt

Use the reference check to explore areas that you are unclear about relating to the candidate. If you're really clear on humility and smarts, probe specifically for hunger. Use the time wisely, and get to questions that reveal specific behaviors rather than general assessments.

Pay Attention to References Who Don't Respond

When reference givers do not respond to your requests for a reference, it is possible that they aren't enthusiastic about the candidate. Remember, the candidate provided the names of the references. Most people are excited to provide a positive reference for a former employee or colleague. When they aren't, they often delay or avoid doing so.

Ask What Others Would Say

Just as you would ask the candidate what others would say about him or her, ask references the same question. It gives them permission to say, "I always thought she was a hard worker, but some of her colleagues weren't so sure." That allows them to feel like they aren't bad-mouthing the candidate, but at the same time makes it easier to share important information.

APPLICATION #2: ASSESSING CURRENT EMPLOYEES

Another extremely important application of the ideal team player model is the assessment or evaluation of current employees. In the end, there are three outcomes of this evaluation: (1) confirming that the employee is an ideal team player, (2) helping the employee improve and become one, or (3) deciding to move the employee out.

Thankfully, humility, hunger, and smarts are not inherent traits, but rather they can be adopted by people with the desire to embrace them. Leaders can evaluate their people against the three virtues in order to help them identify what they need to work on for their own good and the good of the team. This is the preferred outcome.

However, there will be situations in which a leader is struggling with an employee, and the assessment can be used to identify the source of that struggle: a lack of humility, hunger, or smarts. If the employee is unwilling or unable to address the shortcoming, dismissal may be the best outcome for the employee and the team.

What happens when a manager can't decide if an employee has the will or ability to improve? My preference, and my recommendation, is to err on the side of caution and keep working with the employee. Why? Because I believe it is a tragedy to lose an employee for the wrong reasons. Not only does it create an unnecessarily painful situation for that person, but it also robs the team of a potentially valuable contributor.

It's important not to misread my advice as permission to tolerate people who don't fit. Too often, leaders know that an employee really doesn't belong and would be better elsewhere, and they fail to act because they lack courage. This is neither wise nor virtuous. My suggestion here only applies to situations in which a leader is sincerely unsure about the employee's ability to improve and change.

So how exactly should a leader go about evaluating people for humility, hunger, and smarts? There is no easy, quantitative diagnostic, but there are reliable, qualitative approaches that can work very well.

Manager Assessment

There are a number of questions managers can ask themselves about a given employee to determine whether he or she is humble, hungry, or smart. Here are some good ones.

Humble

Does he genuinely compliment or praise teammates without hesitation?

Does she easily admit when she makes a mistake?

Is he willing to take on lower-level work for the good of the team?

Does she gladly share credit for team accomplishments?

Does he readily acknowledge his weaknesses?

Does she offer and receive apologies graciously?

Hungry

Does he do more than what is required in his own job?

Does she have passion for the "mission" of the team?

Does he feel a sense of personal responsibility for the overall success of the team?

Is she willing to contribute to and think about work outside of office hours?

Is he willing and eager to take on tedious and challenging tasks whenever necessary?

Does she look for opportunities to contribute outside of her area of responsibility?

Smart

Does he seem to know what teammates are feeling during meetings and interactions?

Does she show empathy to others on the team?

Does he demonstrate an interest in the lives of teammates?

Is she an attentive listener?

Is he aware of how his words and actions impact others on the team?

Is she good at adjusting her behavior and style to fit the nature of a conversation or relationship?

An ideal team player will merit a "yes" answer to almost every one of these questions. If that seems unrealistic, go back and look at the questions again and imagine which of them would be unnecessary or optional. And remember, we're looking for ideal team players, not adequate ones.

The purpose of using these questions is not to provide leaders with a definitive, quantitative indicator of humility, hunger, or people smarts, but rather to inform their judgment and intuition. In many cases, a leader will have an intuitive sense of how an employee stacks up against the three virtues without having to do an assessment at all. In those situations, the assessment can serve as a helpful check of that intuition.

Employee Self-Assessment

I believe that the most effective way to assess employees is often to ask them to evaluate themselves. Certainly, this is not always the case. Some employees—the ones who lack people smarts in a *big* way—may not even be aware of it. Those who are *not at all* humble will often lack the self-esteem to admit it. And the people who are *clearly not* hungry would be too embarrassed to admit their relative lack of passion or commitment to a team.

Having said that, the vast majority of employees really are willing to own up to their limitations, as long as the process is aimed at improvement instead of punishment and assuming that the work environment is not completely dysfunctional. This self-assessment approach is preferable because it allows employees to take ownership for their areas of development, and it minimizes the possibility of defensiveness and denial.

The best way to allow employees to do self-assessments is to give them explicit questions to consider, and phrase those questions in ways that encourage honesty. Ironically, as is true for interviews, the best way to do that is to ask employees to assess what their teammates would say about them. It's still a self-assessment, but it is based on observable behaviors. After all, a good team player must not only have the right attitude, but must demonstrate the right behaviors in a way that others see and understand.

Instructions:

Use the scale below to indicate how each statement applies to your actions on the team. Respond as honestly as possible, as this will allow you to most accurately identify any areas of development that you may have.

Scale:

3 = Usually   2 = Sometimes   1 = Rarely

Humble

My teammates would say:

_____ 1. I compliment or praise them without hesitation.

_____ 2. I easily admit to my mistakes.

_____ 3. I am willing to take on lower-level work for the good of the team.

_____ 4. I gladly share credit for team accomplishments.

_____ 5. I readily acknowledge my weaknesses.

_____ 6. I offer and accept apologies graciously.

_____ **Total Humility Score**

Hungry

My teammates would say:

_____ 7. I do more than what is required in my own job.

_____ 8. I have passion for the "mission" of the team.

_____ 9. I feel a sense of personal responsibility for the overall success of the team.

_____ 10. I am willing to contribute to and think about work outside of office hours.

_____ 11. I am willing to take on tedious or challenging tasks whenever necessary.

_____ 12. I look for opportunities to contribute outside of my area of responsibility.

_____ **Total Hunger Score**

Smart
My teammates would say:

_____ 13. I generally understand what others are feeling during meetings and conversations.

_____ 14. I show empathy to others on the team.

_____ 15. I demonstrate an interest in the lives of my teammates.

_____ 16. I am an attentive listener.

_____ 17. I am aware of how my words and actions impact others on the team.

_____ 18. I adjust my behavior and style to fit the nature of a conversation or relationship.

_____ **Total Smart Score**

Scoring:

Remember, the purpose of this tool is to help you explore and assess how you embody the three virtues of an ideal team player. The standards for "ideal" are high. An ideal team player will have few of these statements answered with anything lower than a '3' (usually) response.

- A score of 18 or 17 is an indication that the virtue is a potential strength.
- A score range of 16 to 14 is an indication that you most likely have some work to do around that virtue to become an ideal team player.
- A score of 13 or lower is an indication that you need improvement around that virtue to become an ideal team player.

Finally, keep in mind that while this tool is quantitative, the real value will be found in the qualitative, developmental conversations among team-members and their managers. Don't focus on the numbers, but rather the concepts and the individual statements where you scored low.

A Gentler Approach: Ranking

If using an assessment like this seems a little overwhelming given the politics or sensitivity on a team or in a given organization, here is an alternative approach. Ask team members to simply rank the three virtues for themselves, starting with the one they feel they demonstrate most clearly, followed by the second, and then the third. This allows everyone to call out their relative weakness without having to admit the extent of that weakness, and it gives the leader and the employee a place to begin development.

Peer Evaluations versus Peer Discussion

I'm not a big proponent of peer evaluations in general, at least not the formal kind where teammates assess one another's strengths and weaknesses on paper and then learn how they were evaluated at a later date. I think that process is fraught with the potential for misunderstanding, politics, and unnecessary pain.

When it comes to assessing peers on the basis of humility, hunger, or people smarts, my opposition is even stronger. That's because these attributes are particularly personal, and the price of inaccurate evaluation may be the loss of trust on the team. That price is too high, especially when there are better, more constructive ways to help employees understand their areas for development.

Having said that, I believe that the most powerful activity that occurs around any assessment is peer *discussion*. Sitting down as a group and having teammates reveal and discuss their own relative weaknesses related to humble, hungry, and smart is a powerful way to ensure that all of this will lead to change and that teammates will be one another's best coaches. We'll talk about that more in the next section.

APPLICATION #3: DEVELOPING EMPLOYEES WHO ARE LACKING IN ONE OR MORE OF THE VIRTUES

Once a leader (or employee) has established a clear sense of his employees' (or his own) relative strengths and weaknesses related to the three virtues, the process of improvement can begin. But before we get into that, we should take on a few critical and cautionary questions up front.

What Is the Key to Making Development Work? And What Do You Do If It Doesn't?

The most important part of the development process, and the part that is so often missing, is the leader's commitment to constantly "reminding" an employee if she is not yet doing what is needed. Without this, improvement will not occur.

I know this seems very simple. So why don't most managers do it? Because it's uncomfortable. No one likes telling a person for the fifth week in a row that she still isn't working hard enough or isn't dealing with her colleagues in a socially appropriate way. It's unpleasant and awkward, and yet, it's what a manager must do.

When a manager steps up to this challenge, week after week after painful week, one of two things will almost always happen. First, the employee will finally break through, determined not to keep hearing those reminders. She'll reach the top of the hill, so to speak, and make her way to the other side where her humility or hunger or smarts kicks in. When that happens, she'll be in her manager's debt forever.

195

The other likely outcome will be that she will finally decide that being humble or hungry or smart is not her thing, and she'll decide on her own to leave. Hopefully, she'll do so with the guidance and blessing of her manager, and her departure will be seen by everyone as the best way for her to move on in her career. Sometimes she won't have that level of self-confidence, and she'll resent the manager and the team for a while. In either case, she is making the decision herself, and that is good.

There is a third outcome that should happen very rarely. In some cases, an employee decides that she will tolerate the constant reminding from her manager about her issues, and she won't leave. In that case, formal action will be necessary to move her off the team, and that's usually a bureaucratic and painful process for everyone.

Some might say, "Hey, that happens all the time in my company!" The reason why nasty terminations and even lawsuits happen in so many organizations is that managers stop reminding people that they aren't living up to expectations. In most situations, here's how it works.

The manager tells her difficult employee that he needs to change—to become more hungry, let's say. Then she sees him slacking off, and maybe she reminds him once. Then she sees it again, and she complains to her husband, or to her colleagues, or worse yet to other members of the team she leads. This goes on for weeks or months, with passive-aggressive comments here and there, until she's finally had enough. Then she sits down with the employee and announces that he's going to be let go, and he seems shocked. Yes, shocked. How can this be?

Well, in the mind of the manager, this guy has been told and he knows that he's not hungry enough. In the mind of the employee, he feels like he was told once, maybe twice, and that he hasn't heard any other complaints so he must be doing okay. He's mad. She's mad. Her boss is mad. The outside attorneys are busy and happy. And the team is in disarray.

Again, the solution is to constantly, repeatedly, kindly, constantly (yes, I said it twice) let the employee know that he's got to get better. Trust me. He'll almost always get better or opt out on his own. But this cannot happen, and it will not happen, if the manager shirks her responsibility to tell him where he stands.

What about Ideal Team Players? Don't They Need Development, Too?

Most of this development section is focused on helping people who lack one of the three virtues in a significant way. But even people who aren't terribly deficient can benefit from improving one or more of the virtues in their lives. And because they're hungry, they're probably going to be looking for ways to improve anyway.

The key to doing this is to make it clear that it is not a punitive exercise and that just because a teammate is relatively lower in one virtue than another does not mean she's not an ideal team player. Ideal, in the context of this book, does not mean perfect.

Once everyone understands that it is merely a developmental opportunity, the best approach is often to use other ideal team members as a stable of coaches. Consider that some members of a team are going to be stronger at humility

197

than others. Get them to coach the ones who would like to improve in this area. The same is true for hungry and smart. When every ideal team player is coaching and being coached, the development process not only improves team members individually, but it also creates a stronger sense of commitment and accountability for the entire team.

Using the self-assessment on page 192–193 of this book is a good way to get started. Ideal team players enjoy analyzing themselves and one another in order to change their behavior and improve their performance.

Okay, let's get back to the purpose of this section, which is helping people who are decidedly lacking in humility, hunger, or smarts. There is no single best way to go about this, as every person has a different set of causes and behavioral manifestations related to his or her weaknesses as a team member. However, there are a number of approaches that I would recommend.

Developing Humility

Humility is the most sensitive of the three virtues, which is why the process of improving in this area is often the most psychologically nuanced. That's because the source of a lack of humility is always related in some way to insecurity, and for most people, insecurity is rooted in childhood and family issues that go way back beyond their first day on the job or the team.

Now, all of us are insecure in one way or another. It's important that someone trying to improve his capacity for humility understands this, otherwise he's likely to feel too ashamed or overwhelmed to begin. If a manager or coach can demonstrate his or her own challenges with humility, it makes it a lot easier for an employee to do so.

Identifying Root Causes

Without getting too deep into psychological analysis or therapy, a manager or coach (or a motivated employee on her own) can experience significant relief simply by identifying the general cause of insecurity. It may have been a lack of support from parents or a traumatic experience in her career or personal life. Whatever the case, it is often extremely helpful for a person to admit, to herself, her manager or even teammates, where her struggle with humility comes from. This alone can greatly improve her ability to be coached and to elicit empathy and grace from colleagues.

Sometimes the cause of struggle with humility, or with the other virtues, can be traced back to an employee's personality type. Using the Myers-Briggs or DISC profiles, for instance, it is sometimes possible to predict which people might have a higher likelihood of having humility problems. Pointing this out to an employee can be another big source of relief, as it allows him to realize that he is not a bad person and that many others with his same type share his challenge. It also gives him a somewhat objective rationale that he can explain to colleagues. Of course, it's not an excuse, but rather an explanation that provides the context for going forward.

Exposure Therapy

Beyond identifying and admitting the cause of their challenge, people who lack humility need behavioral training in an exposure therapy kind of way. Don't be put off by the clinical sound of this. What I mean is that employees can make progress simply by acting like they are humble. By intentionally forcing themselves to compliment others, admit their mistakes and weaknesses, and take an interest in colleagues, employees can begin to experience the liberation of humility. This happens because they suddenly realize that focusing on others does not detract from their own happiness, but rather adds to it. After all, humility is the most attractive and central of all virtues.

Let me repeat this, because it's as simple as it is important. What we're talking about here is simply having employees practice the very behaviors that they struggle with, so that they can come to understand the benefits to themselves and others. One way to make this happen is for the employee to make a list of the desired behaviors related to their area of development and then track their own actions over a period of time. Sometimes having a manager involved in that process is helpful for the purposes of encouragement and verification.

But the best way of all is to have teammates coach the employee, providing encouragement and immediate feedback when the desired virtues are demonstrated or lacking. If this sounds corny or childish, it is anything but that. There is nothing like having a teammate say, "Hey, I really appreciate that you've been so encouraging lately. And your concern for me personally has made a real difference." I would challenge anyone who hears that from a colleague to claim that it doesn't make him want to continue that behavior.

Similarly, it's pretty powerful when a teammate kindly says, "Hey, I think you're doing that bragging thing again, and you asked us to help you by letting you know when we see it." When an entire team agrees to help an open-minded teammate, even in an area as seemingly sensitive as humility, it is amazing the progress that can be made.

Leader Modeling

Another important aspect of development for an employee is knowing that his manager values humility and does her best to demonstrate it. Even if the manager struggles, her willingness to admit it and continue working on it will go a long way toward encouraging the employee to do the same. This is true with all of the virtues, as well as in any other behavioral pursuit related to work.

Developing Hunger

Hunger is the least sensitive and nuanced of the three virtues. That's the good news. The bad news is, based on my experience, it's the hardest to change.

While it's tempting for an employee to downplay his lack of hunger, it's difficult for him to deny it over time because of the behaviorally observable, and often measurable, nature of the virtue. From work rate and output to goal achievement and hours worked, it's not hard to demonstrate to an employee that he seems less hungry than his colleagues.

Unfortunately, even when he acknowledges a problem in this area, getting him to actually become hungry is difficult. Remember, it's not merely a matter of increasing his output. There are plenty of methods and tools related to goal setting and performance management for doing that. It's about actually transforming the employee so that he can ultimately come to embody the idea of going above and beyond and no longer need extra prodding and reminding.

Why is this so difficult? I suppose it's because a person who lacks hunger sometimes prefers to be this way, at least in the specific context of a given team. In other words, for some people, being less hungry than others has its benefits. More free time. Less responsibility. More emphasis on other, more preferred activities. That isn't to say that someone who prefers these things is a bad person. But quite often, he is a bad team member. (Yes, I know that sounds politically incorrect, but it's true. Plenty of fun, talented, and friendly people aren't great team players at work because their hunger is directed at activities outside of their jobs.)

Compare hunger to the other two virtues, humility and people smarts. Unlike hunger, no one really prefers to lack humility, as this inevitably causes pain and suffering for him or her and those around them. Only the most self-delusional person would claim that lacking humility is a benefit. Deep down inside, we all know it's miserable.

The same is true about being smart. No one would intentionally choose to have a lack of social awareness or interpersonal adeptness. The costs of not being smart, from embarrassment to unintended insensitivity, are great, and there are no benefits.

Lacking hunger, on the other hand, can actually be a desired characteristic for some people. But not for everyone. Plenty of people who lack hunger would like nothing more than to be fully engaged and more productive in their work. The point here is that some people actually do seem to prefer a sense of detachment and routineness, and pouring into them is not going to yield significant returns.

The key is to find out which people who lack hunger really like being that way and which don't, and then to support the ones who want to change, and to lovingly help the others find a job that doesn't require hunger.

Passion for the Mission and the Team

The first and most important part of helping that person become hungry is to find a way to connect her to the importance of the work being done. Until this is accomplished, a manager cannot expect much change.

All too often, employees struggle to become hungry because they don't understand the connection between what they do and the impact it has on others, be they customers, vendors, or other employees. Asking someone to be a more engaged and invested team member won't do much if that employee doesn't think the work she does matters to someone. And no, wanting to keep her job isn't the kind of motivation that turns a lethargic employee into a lively one.

The most effective way to do this is as a team. When a slightly non-hungry employee hears his colleagues describe their motivation and connection to the mission, one of two good things is likely to happen. He may get "infected" by his teammates' passion, and even if that doesn't happen, he may come to realize that he plays an important role in helping them fulfill their passion. Only a truly non-hungry person could be exposed to all of that and remain unaffected.

Clear Expectations

Another indispensable part of developing hunger in an employee (assuming he or she has the required tools and skills) is to set clear behavioral expectations for them and then hold them accountable for those expectations. Yes, that sounds

203

ridiculously obvious, but for those who aren't hungry, it is particularly critical. But while it is also important to set performance targets and goals for these people, it's even more vital to clarify the behaviors you want from them.

For instance, it's one thing to specify how much production you expect from someone in order for her to keep her job. Even a non-hungry employee will often meet the minimum requirement. It's another thing entirely to tell her that you expect her to help her colleagues make their numbers by doing whatever they need, including taking on some additional responsibilities, working more hours (assuming that's possible given her life situation), or doing additional research into problems until they are solved.

An employee who prefers not to be hungry will recoil at this, either immediately or as soon as she sees that she is going to be held accountable for the behavior. Again, if this is the case, she should be lovingly helped to find a job somewhere that doesn't require her to be hungry. There are plenty of places and opportunities that don't require much hunger. But an employee who deep down inside wants to be hungry will respond to the clearer expectations with resolve, warranting the coaching and support of her manager and teammates.

Not-Too-Gentle Reminders

Even an employee with a strong but latent sense of hunger will not be transformed immediately. Habits of lethargy often have been instilled over time, and thus, require some time to break. To make that happen, managers and teammates will need to overcome their reticence to call out a non-hungry teammate when they see behaviors that he needs to change.

Waiting until a performance review to tell him that he isn't doing enough to help the team or including that information in an annual three-hundred-sixty-degree feedback program is not only irresponsible, but cruel.

What that employee needs is someone to give him immediate and unambiguous feedback so that he can quickly digest the pain and translate it into a desire for change. And this needs to happen again and again, perhaps every day for a while, until the behavior changes. Yes, this will require tactful encouragement, support, and patience during the initial stages; otherwise, the well-intentioned team member may be tempted to give up. But in most cases of personal development, tough love is the answer. And though most leaders understand this theoretically, they all too often try to go about it by omitting either the toughness or the love, or sometimes both.

Encouragement

Which brings us to the next piece of obvious but often overlooked advice. When a non-hungry employee starts to exhibit signs of hunger, praise her publicly and have teammates do the same. Might she be slightly embarrassed? Who cares! Will it seem like you're rewarding her for behavior that is merely expected of everyone else? Yes, but she needs it more than anyone else, and they know it. Over time, this extra encouragement and commendation will not be necessary. But until hunger becomes a natural part of her behavioral tool set, keep it coming. And remember, the ones trying to be humble or smart will need their own extra encouragement, too. If you have employees who resent the special attention these people are getting, you might want to assess whether they are truly humble.

205

Leader Modeling

As I wrote in the previous section, an important aspect of development for an employee is knowing that her manager is hungry and that he does his best to demonstrate it. Even if the manager struggles with being hungry at times, his willingness to admit it and continue working on it goes a long way toward helping the employee to do the same.

Developing Smarts

Helping someone become "smarter" about people is not quite as sensitive as humility and, depending on the person, is not quite as hard as hunger, because anyone who lacks in this area most likely wants to improve. Still, it's a challenge.

The key to helping someone become smarter is to make it clear, to everyone involved, that a deficiency in this area is not about intention. Employees who lack people smarts have no desire to create interpersonal problems with their teammates. They just don't understand the nuances of interpersonal situations, and they don't seem to realize how their words and actions impact others. If that person and his teammates know this and remind themselves about it, the process of helping him become smarter will be much easier and more effective.

If teammates slip into the false belief that he is really trying to be a difficult person for some ulterior motive, they are likely to start resenting him and, worse yet, shying away from giving him the help he needs.

Basic Training

A person who has trouble being smart with people can be likened to a pet. Stay with me here; it's not that bad. Like a puppy being trained, he needs to be quickly and lovingly rapped on the nose with a newspaper whenever he does something non-smart. I mean it when I say quickly and lovingly.

Remember, his intentions aren't bad. So, in the middle of a meeting, stop and say, "Hey, Bob, this is the part in the meeting where you should thank her for what she did." Or even, "Bob, I'm going to tell you this because I know you want to know, not because I'm mad at you. I'm kind of bummed out about my family situation, and it would help if you acknowledged it." Or how about this one: "The next time you have an issue with my team, you might not want to send an e-mail, and if you do, run it by someone who can help you put a nice greeting and closing at the beginning and end. My staff was really annoyed last night, but I explained that you didn't mean it that way."

If this sounds rudimentary or even juvenile, that's okay. It won't be once you establish the real nature of the help your employee needs. And if he is sincerely interested in getting better, he'll thank you for it. In fact, it will become a source of humor and bonding for him and the team. After all, his intentions are good. Like a puppy, he'll come to love you for it, and he'll be glad you don't have to clean up after him.

APPLICATION #4: EMBEDDING THE MODEL INTO AN ORGANIZATION'S CULTURE

I believe that teamwork is not a virtue, but rather a choice. It's a strategic decision and an intentional one, which means that it's not for everyone.

Having said that, I must admit that it's hard for me to imagine a company not wanting to experience the benefits of teamwork. But, if the leaders of an organization are not willing to put in the considerable time and effort that it takes to make teamwork more than just a throwaway phrase or break room poster, then there is actually something virtuous about being up front about that.

I say that because I wouldn't want a leader to do what I'm going to recommend here if he or she isn't really committed to a culture of teamwork—the kind that attracts ideal team players. So, for those organizations that are sincere about humility, hunger, and smarts, here are a few simple ideas for embedding those virtues into your culture.

Be Explicit and Bold

Leaders who believe teamwork is important and expect their people to be humble, hungry, and smart should come right out and say so. They should tell everyone. Employees. Vendors. Partners. Customers. Prospective customers. Prospective employees. Everyone.

Of course, they should do this in an appropriate way. It's not marketing that I'm talking about, but rather expectation-setting. The point is to inform anyone who is going to be dealing with the organization, team, or department that they should expect the people they meet to be humble, hungry, and smart.

Leaders shouldn't be cheesy about this. Posters and T-shirts aren't usually the answer. But whatever they do, they shouldn't hide their commitment to the three virtues, and they shouldn't make it easy for humble, hungry, and smart to fade. Eventually, their customers, vendors, partners, and employees will become their best marketing tools for finding the kind of people who fit the organization and for warding off people who don't.

Why aren't more organizations explicit and bold about their culture of teamwork? In many cases, they aren't serious enough about it to put it out there with confidence or integrity. Sometimes they're embarrassed because it might sound corny. Or they think it's too simple. You know what kinds of organizations are explicit about building a strong culture? The successful ones. They're more than willing to do things that are simple or that might elicit cynical or sarcastic responses from competitors. Just ask Southwest Airlines, Chick-fil-A, Ritz-Carlton, or REI.

Catch and Revere

Leaders who want to create a culture of humility, hunger, and people smarts in their organization should be constantly on the lookout for any displays of those virtues. And when they see those displays, they should hold them up as examples for everyone to see.

All too often in life, we see people do what we want them to do and we say nothing, assuming that the behavior has become natural for them, an easy standard. We justify our lack of praise by claiming that it would be embarrassing to the employee to call attention to a behavior that she sees as something fundamental. What we're failing to realize is that the point of praise is not only to reinforce the behavior in that employee, but also to reinforce it in everyone else.

Great team leaders won't be afraid to call out a simple act of teamwork when they see it. They'll acknowledge an act of humility, hunger, or people smarts not because they want to be seen as sophisticated or clever managers, but because they want everyone to know exactly what kinds of behavior they expect and appreciate.

I've found that, in most cases, managers greatly underestimate the impact that a comment or quick gesture of approval has on employees. They'll spend weeks trying to tweak an annual bonus program or some other compensation system, believing that their employees are coin-operated, but they'll neglect to stop someone during a meeting and say, "Hey, that's a fantastic example of hunger. We should all try to be more like that."

I'm not saying that compensation doesn't matter. But if we want to create a culture of humility, hunger, and smarts, the best way to do it is to constantly be catching people exhibiting those virtues and publicly holding them up as examples. No balloons, pastries, or plastic tchotchkes are necessary, just genuine, in-the-moment appreciation.

Detect and Address

The last simple step in embedding humility, hunger, and smarts into your organization is something that any parent or coach would tell you is critical (even if it's hard for them to put it into practice). Whenever you see a behavior that violates one of the values, take the time to let the violator know that his behavior is out of line. And don't just do it in egregious situations. Often, the smaller offenses are the ones that are harder for employees to see and the ones they learn from the most.

Of course, doing this well requires tact and good judgment. Coming down too hard on a minor error, or being too gentle with a blatant one, creates its own problems. Having said that, the key is that leaders and, eventually, teammates don't squander opportunities for constructive learning. Great cultures tend to be appropriately intolerant of certain behaviors, and great teams should be quick and tactful in addressing any lack of humility, hunger, and people smarts.

CONNECTING THE IDEAL TEAM PLAYER MODEL WITH THE FIVE DYSFUNCTIONS OF A TEAM

ome who have read *The Five Dysfunctions of a Team* might be wondering how that book and model fit with this one. Some of those same readers may have even been involved in consulting or training activities around the five dysfunctions model, and they might be curious as to whether the ideal team player model can help them improve upon the work they've done.

I am glad to say that the two models compliment one another. Here's how.

First, *The Five Dysfunctions of a Team* book, online team assessment, and other products all focus on how a group of people must interact in order to become a cohesive team. This book, however, focuses on an individual team member and the virtues that make him or her more likely to overcome the dysfunctions that derail teams.

For instance, a person who grows in humility is going to be much better at demonstrating vulnerability than a person who is arrogant, insecure, and egotistical. Similarly, a person who improves in people smarts will have an easier time engaging in productive conflict, knowing how to read and understand teammates, and adjusting words and behaviors appropriately.

In other words, the ideal team player is all about the makeup of individual team members, while the five dysfunctions are about the dynamics of teams getting things done.

Second, any team that has invested time and energy in the five dysfunctions methodology can use the humble, hungry, smart model as a tune-up. We've found that some teams hit a wall in their progress overcoming the dysfunctions. In many cases, the team can break through that wall by having team members go deeper into their individual development around the virtues that might be holding them back.

It's like a race car engine that has plenty of gasoline and oil, but a little bit of additive can make it run more effectively and efficiently, lubricating moving parts better or making fuel more combustible. (Okay, that's the limit of my automotive knowledge, but you probably get the point.) When team members improve their abilities to be humble, hungry, or smart, they'll be able to make more progress in overcoming the five dysfunctions on a regular basis.

Finally, the ideal team player model and tools presented in this book provide yet another opportunity for team members to be vulnerable with one another. By sitting down and acknowledging their strengths and weaknesses—remember, the leader should always go first—a team can develop greater levels of trust among members, which make conflict, commitment, accountability, and results that much more likely.

213

The Five Dysfunctions of a Team Summary

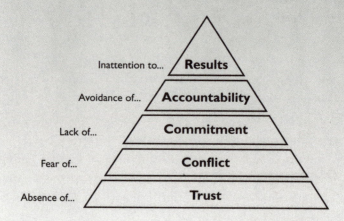

Inattention to... **Results**

Avoidance of... **Accountability**

Lack of... **Commitment**

Fear of... **Conflict**

Absence of... **Trust**

#1: Absence of Trust
The fear of being vulnerable with team members prevents the building of trust within the team.

#2: Fear of Conflict
The desire to preserve artificial harmony stifles the occurrence of productive, ideological conflict.

#3: Lack of Commitment
The lack of clarity and/or the fear of being wrong prevents team members from making decisions in a timely and definitive way.

#4: Avoidance of Accountability
The need to avoid interpersonal discomfort prevents team members from holding one another accountable for their behaviors.

#5: Inattention to Results
The desire for individual credit erodes the focus on collective success.

For more information about the model or anything else relating to the five dysfunctions, go to www.tablegroup.com.

A FINAL THOUGHT—
BEYOND WORK TEAMS

Over the past twenty years, it has become clear to me that humility, hunger, and people smarts have relevance outside of the workplace. A humble, hungry, and smart spouse, parent, friend, or neighbor is going to be a more effective, inspiring, and attractive person—one that draws others to them and serves others better.

But I must admit that apart from the other two virtues, humility stands alone. It is, indeed, the greatest of all virtues and the antithesis of pride, which is the root of all sin, according to the Bible. The most compelling example of humility in the history of mankind can be found in Christ, who humbled himself to share in our humanity. He attracted people of all kinds when he walked the earth, and continues to do so today, providing an example of humility that is as powerful as it is countercultural.

And so, it is my hope that readers of this book will take something else away with them and apply it in their lives: an appreciation for the true gift that it is to be humble and the divine origins of that virtue.

MORE RESOURCES

If you'd like more information about the ideal team player model, visit our web site at www.tablegroup.com/idealteamplayer.

You'll find the following resources there:

- Video clips
- Employee self-assessment
- Manager assessment
- Related articles
- Model graphic
- Author Q&A
- Other tools and resources

If you'd like someone to help you implement any of the concepts in this book, please contact us at The Table Group by calling 925–299–9700, or visit www.tablegroup.com.

ACKNOWLEDGMENTS

I want to acknowledge and thank my wonderful wife, Laura, and four lovable boys, Matthew, Connor, Casey, and Michael, for giving me just enough time and space I need to write books. And I thank my teammates at The Table Group—Amy, Tracy, Karen, Jeff, Lynne, Jackie, Kim, Cody, and Dani—for being part of a living laboratory in humility, hunger, and people smarts.

Thanks to my fantastic agent, Jim Levine, for your commitment to and insights around the ideal team player model. And to all the terrific people at Wiley for your partnership and commitment to me and The Table Group over all these years.

I want to thank all of the consultants around the world for dedicating themselves to helping clients make organizational health a reality. And I'm grateful to all the clients interested in organizational health who trust us to serve them with our products and services.

Special thanks to my friends at ViNE and The Amazing Parish movement, as well as the dear Carmelite sisters in Los Angeles and my many priest friends spread around the country, for your prayers and support. Thanks to Matthew Kelly for reminding me to write this book.

And thanks, Mom, for your daily prayers and concern, which I cherish. And to my late father: thank you for being my first coach and teacher of teamwork.

And of course, all thanks are due to God; You are the source of all that is good.

ABOUT THE AUTHOR

Patrick Lencioni is founder and president of The Table Group, a firm dedicated to helping leaders improve their organizations' health since 1997. His principles have been embraced by leaders around the world and adopted by organizations of virtually every kind including multinational corporations, entrepreneurial ventures, professional sports teams, the military, nonprofits, schools, and churches.

Lencioni is the author of ten business books with over five million copies sold worldwide. His work has appeared in the *Wall Street Journal, Harvard Business Review, Fortune, Bloomberg Businessweek,* and *USA Today,* among other publications.

Prior to founding The Table Group, Lencioni served as an executive at Sybase Inc. He started his career at Bain & Company and later worked at Oracle Corporation.

Lencioni lives in the San Francisco Bay Area with his wife and their four sons.

To learn more about Patrick and The Table Group, please visit www.tablegroup.com.

table group

Patrick Lencioni is founder of The Table Group, a firm
dedicated to changing the world of work. The Table Group
provides executives, team leaders, managers and employees
with everything they need to make their organizations
healthier, teams more cohesive, and people
more engaged and fulfilled.

www.**Table**Group.com

VISIT OUR
WEBSITE & EXPLORE:

CONSULTING

SPEAKING

BOOKS

PRODUCTS

FREE RESOURCES

PODCAST